Signature Collection

Volume 2

Maxine Spyres Hixon

Signature Collection

Volume 2

Maxine Spyres Hixon

Published by:
Brentwood Christian Press
P. O. Box 4773
Columbus, Georgia 31914-4773
(800) 334-8861
www.brentwoodbooks.com

Poetry Collections by Maxine:

Sand and Pearls
Voice of the Heart
Poetic Potpourri
Mither
Rhymes of the Time (a children's book – which was a collaborative work with her daughters)
Hidden Treasure I
Hidden Treasure II
Hidden Treasure III
Wealth of Wisdom
Signature Collection I

One of Maxine's favorite Bible scripture verses:

Deuteronomy 31:6

"Be strong and of a good courage,
fear not, nor be afraid of them:
For the Lord thy God, he it is that doth go with thee;
he will not fail thee, nor forsake thee."

Table of Contents

SALVATION

COMFORT, HOPE and INSPIRATION

5

DOCTRINAL and DIDACTIC

POETIC FORMS

THOUGHT PONDERING

7

SEASONAL and OCCASIONAL

Nature

8

NOSTALGIA and ROMANCE

HOME and FAMILY LIFE

POLITICAL

Dedication

TO: All of Maxine's avid readers out there, we are pleased to present this "poetic smorgasbord!"

Foreword

As we come to the close of our literary journey with our late Mother, Maxine Spyres Hixon, with this, her last collection of poetry, we come with mixed emotions – happy to see her work to completion, and her books now to be handed down for posterity, yet, we feel a poignancy and bitter-sweetness, also. Our hope and prayer is that her poetry continues to bless countless lives.

Maxine leaves a rich legacy, that addresses topics with a wide range of diversity. She was versatile, as one can tell by the wide variety of subjects she chose to write about. With Maxine at your side, sharing jewels of wisdom, with God's help you can overcome any difficulty you encounter in life. One church lady, while reading Mother's poetry in church aloud, said that "her poetry was how she made it through each day." And that's a compliment indeed, for her poems are powerful! Maxine was a mighty prayer warrior. We, her family, couldn't think of a better support system for us than to have Mother "in our corner" praying for us.

Maxine held to a high standard of ideals and values. She remained undaunted in spirit, had an indomitable spirit, and was a woman of courage and faith. She held to sound principles. Two of our favorites quotes of hers were, "For every problem God provides the remedy," and the Bible verse, "Be of good courage and the Lord will strengthen your heart."

Mother had the patience of Job, the spirit of Mary, who sat and learned at Jesus' Feet, and the fortitude of Deborah. Of her it can be said, "When God made 'you,' He broke the mold." For there's been no one like her, before or since, who compares. She not only talked the talk, but walked the walk.

And so we find ourselves in this final phase of publishing with yet another promising collection, chocked full and brimming with inspiration. She is a true author of great merit, and stands in her own right, among the very greatest. We're especially glad to share her poetry with family, friends, her church family, residents and staff of Nursing Homes, Veteran's Homes, our local Newspaper and Internet, various Anthologies, and the Nation's top fifty colleges and universities.

Maxine understood the psychology of mankind. She offers a Bible-based spiritual approach to God's psychology so much needed in today's times. Be sure to ponder her "Thought-Provoking" poems where she addresses problems for troubled people. So much of psychology today is the influence of the Oriental East on the Western thought, and of those who don't claim any love for God or Jesus. These two opposing systems of thought make for a great disparity, as inspirational spirit-based writings remain mostly nonexistent and even silent concerning mankind's eternal destiny. And yet, God, in His Word, promises to give "power and love and a sound mind." When one turns his soul into God's Hands for safekeeping, he has an inner peace and security that this world cannot take away.

May your lives be truly blessed, as have ours – for we can say Maxine's nine volumes of inspirational poetry, not including *Mither* and *Rhymes of the Times*, that they all have been a joy to compile. Just conversing daily with Mother, through her written words – has brought us happiness beyond all measure.

If only one soul comes to the saving knowledge of Jesus Christ, through this testimony and witness, or some soul is helped by her writing, she would deem it all worthwhile.

May her light continue to be a beacon in the night for the generations to come, because we know in Heaven she now shines as a star in God's firmament, as the Bible tells us of those who win souls. In her lifetime, she turned many to Jesus and onto the paths of righteousness.

She left us with this rich legacy of poetry, and an undying love for her family and her God – that naught of earth stood between.

May God keep you is our prayer,

So until we meet in Heaven's bright tomorrow,
    We bid you a fond farewell,

Tena M. Hixon and Pamela Hixon Rhea
(Maxine's two daughters)

Biography

Maxine Spyres was born on January 29, 1926 in Adair County, Stilwell, Oklahoma. She was valedictorian of her eighth grade class, and finished high school a year early. She married Carl W. Hixon on October 6, 1945 in Selma, California. They have four children: Tena, Pamela, Ronald, and Rodney.

Maxine attended the Northeastern State Teacher's College in Tahlequah, Oklahoma. She taught school during World War II in a one-room schoolhouse – children of all ages. Maxine was also a Real Estate Broker for many years.

Maxine's collection of inspirational poetry published in recent years are *Sand and Pearls, Voice of the Heart, Mither*, (a collection of one hundred twenty-two poems, written in its entirety after Maxine suffered a left-side paralysis stroke,) *Poetic Potpourri, Hidden Treasure (Volumes I and II, & III,) Wealth of Wisdom, Signature Collection 1*, and this, her final volume, *Signature Collection II*. In 1995, Maxine collaborated with her two daughters, to write a children's book, *Rhymes of the Times* published in 2015, which she illustrated.

Maxine's poems have been published in their hometown *Log Cabin Democrat* for over forty-five years. Many of her poems have won prizes in poetry contests, been published in anthologies, and are on the Internet.

Maxine and her family made their home in Conway, Arkansas, for over thirty-eight years, where her two daughters continue to reside.

This volume, *Signature Collection II*, completes nine volumes of religious poetry, not including the children's rhyme book, and the book, *Mither*, written after having a stroke. Maxine passed from this life on, December 2, 2006, exactly seven months and seven days after suffering a massive stroke. Her daughters have published her works posthumously.

Her works will continue live on in the hearts and minds of her many readers, whose lives will be made richer for the reading.

Salvation

Jesus Died For Our Sin

Jesus died for my sin;
Once was enough – He never has to do it again,
He can be your Saviour the same as mine;
He died for you at the same time.
He can be Saviour to you the
    the same as He is to me.
He knows all – who to Him belong,
And can call them all by name.
He knows everything we do, say, or think –;
He lovingly watches every move we make.
In peace we abide in His loving care;
Though troubles come full circle ... He's there –
Our troubles and cares to bear.
Since a girl, my Saviour had a place in my heart,
So many years ago; He never will depart.
Life with Him has peace in troubled times,
Because His loving kindness is sufficient we find.
It matters not circumstances, for I belong to Him,
    and He belongs to me.
He can be the same to you in your heart.
In the sunshine or in the storms,
He does His part; He's always there.
When you're young, and when you're old,
He always there – at Calvary, He paid for your soul.

God is Love

God is love ... no better way to say it.
   "For God so loved the world that He gave His
Only Begotten Son – that whoever believeth
In Him should not perish, but have
Everlasting life" ...
Man can search and work – his sins he can't remit,
Plans for redemption other than God's, is rife.
Anything other than God's plan leads to hell – the pit!
(Causing much heartache and strife.)
If the human race would accept God's plan in the Holy
   Writ,
The whole world would be saved and revived!

You Choose

Each person draws ever near ...
When there shall be time no more;
The trumpet sound ... all will hear;
Death may overtake before.

To the last days, the world's geared;
Each generation's closer still:
God's judgment needs to be feared;
Without Christ ... man's work is nil!

The living know they shall die:
While Hell hath enlarged itself ...
To meet thee at thy coming;
Rejecting Christ ... Hell is left.

God made man with the power of choice;
Accept or reject Christ ...
Decision man makes, his voice,
At Calvary, Christ paid sin's price.

Heaven's all joy, peace and love:
Hell is torment forevermore ...
Faith in Christ means life above,
He is Heaven's only door.

Christ Triumphs Over Sin

In the midst of forest fires,
Fire can't go where fire has been.
Ashes left as fire expires ...
Naught is left where it began.

Not one soul will go to Hell,
That's Christ's blood has cleansed from sin:
But, forever with Christ dwell ...
God's plan since the world began.

Fire burns all that's in its path,
Fire can't go where fire has been;
As Christ's blood does stay God's wrath,
Man depraved was born in sin.

On the cross, Christ paid God's price,
For Salvation of the lost ...
Power – in the blood of Christ,
Covers sin at awful cost.

By grace through faith are you saved:
It's a "gift" ... man's "works" have no part;
Christ died for all who believe;
With repentance in their heart.
The fires of Hell have no power –
Where the blood of Christ has been.

Real Comfort

Best stick with the things you know …
Don't be led astray because of some saying so –;
Never change your beliefs just to seem smart,
Or in something untrue you'll likely take part.

Whatever the Bible states will come to pass,
At the end of time, many will be aghast;
God's Word is always the basis
In obeying it, our life can be an oasis.

Put no confidence in the flesh,
But, trust the Lord … heart and spirit will mesh.
Christ, the Saviour, is the Rock of our Salvation;
All man-made plans we're to shun … for useless when
    said and done.

Refusing to accept Christ as Saviour … leaves only Hell,
Those refusing, in the Judgment, all will not be well,
The power of choice God gives to man
Matters not where one lives throughout the land.

According to the Scriptures, time for man is soon
    running out,
If you don't believe it – study will do away with doubt.
God gave His only begotten Son, the sacrifice for sin,
Christ stood as a Lamb slain before time began.

Thankfulness to God for His wonderful gift,
Should be remembered each day – giving hearts a lift,
In the midst of trouble, peace will forever stay,
For the Lord is always there … pointing the way.

Such comfort in knowing Christ as Saviour,
Trusting and believing ... nothing good we have done;
He tells us He always cares for His own,
There is security in knowing we're His ... Heaven's
  our home.

The Religious People Crucified My Saviour

Religious peopled crucified God's Son.
Claiming He was an imposter – and from God didn't come.
The self-righteous Pharisees were stuck on self,
A heart without Christ is of righteousness bereft.
God's Word says our righteousness is "as filthy rags,"
All who refuse to accept Christ – the devil tags.

No matter the reports of "goodness" our own,
The refusal of His Son ... God does not condone.
Water, steam and ice – all three are "H2O"
God the Father, Holy Spirit and the Son ...
Is Heaven's Trinity – three in one God-head;
Those who accept Christ are of the Spirit led.

Pious imposters are out to deceive.
Claiming to "know God," your vote to receive.
"Whosoever denieth the Son, the same
    hath not the Father."
"Who is a liar but he that denieth
That Jesus is the Christ? He is a Antichrist.
That denieth the Father and the Son." (I John 2:22-23)

God, the Father, Son and Holy Spirit are one
Whosoever denieth the Son, the
    same hath not the Father ... he that acknowledgeth
The Son hath the Father also, a triune Godhead.
Thanks be to God, Jesus is alive, not dead!

.

Your Choice

You choose your own way;
Heaven or Hell's wrath;
While on earth you live;
Too late when life's gone;
Death has naught to say;
While day ... choose your path;
Heart to Christ you need to give;
He'll save ... He alone.

Nothing good we've done;
For Heaven to see;
Because of God's love;
We approach His Throne;
Through Jesus, His Son;
Who died to set free;
He's gone on before;
To welcome us home.

Thank You, Lord

Thank you, dear Lord, for answering
    our prayers ...
Thank you, so ... for saving our
    souls –;
Thank you, Lord ... for your promises –
    when with faith we dare ...
When our spirits are right – we
    can rejoice, and be whole.

Burdened with a load of care ...
    but, Christ is always there to share –;
He will make the mountain of
    obstacles run a smooth course.
We only see a little – much of the
    time, it seems – more than we can bear.
Then, when God calls a halt ... things
    will turn aright – with a little of His force.

In it all, God is to be praised – by each
    member of the human race ...
Knowing we're dependent – one and
    all upon His mercy ...
One day, we'll all have to meet Him
    face to face ...
Then will be the Judgment – not mercy –
    when you've seen the last of His grace!

Oh, man of destitute spirit, lowly and
    mean ...
One day, you'll meet your match in
    Hell's fire seen, while on earth you busily tormented.
Claiming to be a Christian ... yet, has
    your soul been redeemed?

Hear the words of old – repent …
for there's a coming day ahead …
when you won't be "so bold."

Heaven or Hell

Heaven or Hell
You have a choice.
When the end will be,
You just can't tell.
Perhaps, around the corner,
Where you can't see.
It's up to you.
You must decide.

Comfort, Hope, and Inspiration

All's Well With My Soul

God is everywhere …
All places the same; …
He cradles the world; …
Caring for my soul, …

My burdens He bears,
Calling me by name.
As my life unfurls;
He's there to behold.

Whether life or death; …
Our God is in charge; …
Absent in body; …
Present with the Lord, …

As long as there's breath;
And in death discharged
Still, all's well with me;
God gives His reward.

Christ is the answer;
To every soul's strife;
Faith … comforts the heart;
Just knowing … God … knows;

Trust … life's enhancer
Secure throughout life;
Because of Christ's part
All's well with my soul.

An Even Place

Our feet walk in an even place - Walking in truth …
never turning back.

When we walk in God's truth … - Feet are on a solid
rock..

Heart on truth does lock. - Though at times, the
devil does attack;

We reap the benefits of God's grace - When old or in our
youth.

When feet stand in an even place - One isn't prone to
slide.

Living for the Lord gains rewards - In truth, running the
Christian race.

The path – even and wide - For truth, our Saviour
died.

Faith

"Faith is the substance of things ... hoped
   for, evidence of things not seen;"
The substance is in the faith ... though
   unseen – the evidence is there;
Things are not always to you and me
   as they may seem ...
Faith is intangible ... yet substance's there, and evidence ...
   for what faith does dare.

God Knows

Men boast of many things ... things accomplished,
    and those perceived ...
But, God looks into all hearts – knowing
    what each one believes –;
God needs no one to report to Him – accusing
    or excusing in many a word;
Everything is as if surfaced in plain sight –
    all deeds and every word is heard –;
Hearts holding secrets – withheld from
    the eyes of man ...
Are viewed extensively by the One who
    holds the world with great power in His Hand.

The moment one believes in the Christ
    Who was sent ...;
Is in that instant made a child of
    God –
with heart broken and rent –;
The angels in Heaven rejoice over one who is
    saved...
A new spiritual heart is given – replacing one
    that was depraved.
We're to work our own Salvation – not work
    for it as some seem to think – heeded –
What's inside the spiritual heart – needs be
    nourished and fed ...

To live for Christ a victorious life –
    over-comers we must be –;
Living lives in compliance with God's
    Holy Word – for every one to see ...
To bring glory to God – by example –
    in word and deed;

Not to exalt self – thoughtless of what
    is right – taking no heed.
In the Day of Judgment – all will be
    brought to light …
Even in this life what one deems obscure –
    many times does shine forth as in the day,
    not dark of night.

Bearing Your Own Burdens and Others

Many hide sad hearts with a smile;
Sadness reaching ... eyes' depth;
Willing to go the extra mile;
In prayer and eyes that weep.

Hearts aching, so burdened with troubles their own;
Yet, they're there when needed;
Concern ... by which their love is shown;
Love's actions preceded.

Such love Christians had long ago ...;
Can it be said of us –;
"My, they do love each other so –;"
To win the lost we must.

Self-centered folk reject what's right;
Care naught save for their own;
In their orbit ... "their" star shines brightly
No other ... they condone.

Faith in Christ binds hearts together;
As troubles come to all ...
One sees himself as debtor –;
Condemned ... on Christ he'll call.

Dreaded?

You hear the word dreaded ... many times
    through life ...
What's dreaded by one – to another is of no
    great concern –;
Dread can disrupt the peace of life ... causing
    much needless strife ...
Much wisdom it takes ... ruing our mistakes –
    trusting the Lord – not dread, but discern.

When we have preconceived ideas as to the
    outcome of disagreeable things ...
Like it or not – we do count God out ...
    even though we pray –;
God can change so many things ... the
    change wrought that faith and prayer brings;
God is in charge – He's over all ... matters
    not what atheists and skeptics say.

When occasions come – you don't know just what
    to do ...
Trust the Lord – His help is ever near – to all who
    have trusted Christ as Saviour –
Staying close to Him ... you will be victorious
    as right you stand for and pursue ...
Most important is to please God, so He's the
    One who looks upon you with favor.

Only Believe

All things are possible to him that
    believeth …
In Christ's name you must … ask with faith …
    help to receive.
We must trust God to provide what's needed
    in life …
Trusting though threads of life, dark with bright
    ones He weaves.

He'll not put more on us than we're
    able to bear:
As the Master Weaver, God knows just what
    we need,
Obeying Him in adversity … we need
    dare:
We should prove our love by faith
    and to His Word pay heed.

In the light of the sun … what is seen
    is not faith:
It's in the dark, black-shadowed
    weavings of the night …
As we walk by faith's shining light
    and not by sight;
We show Christ to the world as its
    only true light.

Heartbroken

Heartbroken ... so sad, why should this be so?
We have a Heavenly Father and Saviour who
    will never let us go ...
All the sadness in a heart ... should we
    ever doubt that He does know –?
He, the One, who made us and did life
    on us bestow ...
We need be strong in faith and ever drawing
    closer to Him, still –
Always praying for His help ... in us
    fulfilling, of His Will.
Others may help, give of their best, but,
    only He can comfort – giving perfect rest.
Many times, things thrust upon us, by someone
    not giving of their best –
God, though long-suffering – is rendering
    them at best ...
A chance to prove themselves ... though
    failing in the past –;
God's Spirit will not always strive with
    man – one time will be the last.
Time can be redeemed – brought back – by working hard
    and fast ...
Though Salvation is a gift – it must be
    received in this life, or the die is cast.
There is a great gulf fixed between Heaven
    and hell – the chasm is vast.

Such Help

We know our only help comes from the Lord;
Though God uses His people to do His work, here on earth.
God will give strength to those who help, and a reward;
All who know Christ as Saviour have a new birth.

It's so comforting to be assured by those who care;
Though we have the promise the Lord will never leave us.
Such a Godly spirit, to have others our burdens
    to help bear –;
With love, they shared our hurt – hearts to adjust.

You feel their love and concern no matter how far away;
The miles separating loved ones matters not in the least ...
Knowing their prayers are ever with you, come what may;
Then God chooses to give relief – just a little of His
    power to release.

Such loving help – doing what they can, and with spiritual
    praying, too –;
Lift such burdens, that without their help, would bend
    you very low.
But, with God's help and such family concern – cares
    not a few...
When there's such dedicated family members and
    God's help – to defeat every foe.

Whatever the trouble – no matter the depths of despair –
Faith in God – loyalty to Christ and those we love,
There's nothing in which we can count God out – never
    would dare.
Hopeless to others – but, not with the Lord – our strength's
    from above.

So many professionals in the health and medical field;
Depend only upon their own expertise and latest
medication.
The Great Physician, (our Lord,) is the One Who can
always heal.
When the maniac of the Gadarenes called upon the Lord,
the Lord regulated his mind,
directing the path to health, defying all medical
regulations.

There were two maniacs of the Gadarenes – cutting
themselves among the tombs,
Jesus came that way; one, only one turned to the Lord …
When he sought Jesus – the demons in his heart and body
had no more room,
Even in his poor tormented mind, he knew, in Jesus, help
he would find.

God Should Be Feared

"The Angel of the Lord encamps all around
Those who fear Him ...
And delivers them" ... He directs a guardian angel
To protect them.

Sin in a life causes trembling and fear, and faith will falter
Turning from God ...
God's Holy Spirit does hearts convict and stir –
Of sin does prod;

Man being a free moral agent, must choose in life
How he will live ...
In choosing this, he chooses how he will die;
His heart to give ...

The valley of death leads to eternity;
Each must travel;
Salvation, by grace through faith ... to ALL is free;
The field's level!

It's level the playing field! ... so many cry
Across our land ...
Christ died on the cross, God's plan, none can defy
Not any man!

It's the choices man makes as to how he lives:
Trusting the Lord ...
Or in doubt, looking to the arm of the flesh,
For his reward.

Repentance and faith toward God – a soul is won;
Christ does the rest ...
Not by works of righteousness which we have done,
... Be it our best.

To be pleasing to God, there has to be faith
Coupled with fear …
God's children who fear Him, as everyone ought;
Angels stay near.

Your Choice

Weighted down beneath a heavy load ...
Shouldering responsibilities down a long crooked road;
But, is that as it should ... or has to be?
Traveling through life midst turns we cannot see –;
No, ... for faith in the Lord is an integral part ...
Coming from a sincere heart.
Looking to God for help – our burdens to bear;
With burdens cast upon Him ... much better we fare.
If bowed beneath life's sin-filled load ...;
It's by choice ... your choosing whatever life's made.
With a load of troubles – bowed to the ground –;
Or lifted by faith ... eyes Heavenward bound

With Love

With love, we do what we do for those
    we care about …
Our hearts are broken along with theirs … when
    we see things going so badly.
God desires the best of us – and will lead
    the way, no doubt;
We need be willing with God's help to –
    ease the pain as best we can – though sad.

Just saying we love – without the deeds to show
    is hard to prove …;
Hearts who love will not stand still – but, work
    while seeking wisdom from above –;
While eager hands with strength from God
    will work, and mountains move;
The scripture says we're to be, "Wise as a serpent and
    harmless as a dove;" – all in the name of love.

Good Thoughts

Good thoughts keep the heart and mind sound.
Right thinking taught in Bible found:
Philippians 4:8 tells us "Whatsoever things are true, honest,
    just, pure, lovely", to think….
Make a good report of virtue and praising,
Else God may give one over to a reprobate mind and heart
(Means not knowing – senses left behind.)
To believe a lie and be damned,
Good thoughts keep the heart and mind sound.
God's children need to keep minds clean,
Pray and upon Him lean.
Prayer and washing by reading of God's
    Word.
With repentance … faith and heart much stirred,
Good thoughts keep the heart and mind sound.

Prayer

In prayer, if we waver in faith, God
    will not hear ...
Nor ... if, we regard iniquity in our
    heart!
God's Word teaches He alone – is the
    one to fear.
Christ is the Way ... in Salvation, works have no part.

By repentance and faith, Christ can be
    your Saviour ...
Salvation is free ... Christ suffered for you and me.
Salvation's by grace through faith ... not
    by works ... in lieu!
A choice you make ...
    choosing is the only part you do;

It's Heaven or Hell, and you will choose
    while living;
God made man ... no puppet, ... but, a free
    moral agent.
Jesus died to save the lost ... His own
    life giving ...
For my sin and your sin He bled and died;
    on the Cross, Christ was rent!

Doctrinal and Didactic

What is it Then?

Down through time, God's men have preached;
The ones God called ... the lost to reach –;
Since Christ organized His Church on the shores of Galilee;
There have been faithful followers to help set souls free.

Preaching God's Word – telling of His saving grace ...
Of how Jesus was sent to die for the human race;
How He died on Calvary's rugged Cross ...;
Saving all who would believe in Him, overcoming sin's
    dross.

The Apostle Paul made tents, and yet preached;
Down through the ages, others have worked to be able to
    preach and teach;
The gifts and callings of God are without repentance;
After a hard day's work – on God's Word, they took
    their stance.

Now as we know it ... in this modern time;
It seems many would listen to stories or rhymes;
God has promised His Holy Spirit will accompany
    His word;
To the convicting of those who hear or have heard.

What is it then, when multitudes come forward;
When scant if any ... scripture is used to "mar" their
    modern gospel.
To be saved, one must believe what Jesus taught while
    here on earth,
By grace, through faith in Him, is Salvation or the
    New Birth.

No Wonder

No wonder the children ... feel neglected
    and alone
Brought in this world – then to be
    left on their own ...;
Did you think ... no one asked to
    be born –
They no more get here ... and
    parents are gone!

Parents will answer to God for the
    care given ... or not ...;
For parents are to be the protectors, providers
    comforters, instructors and friends,
But, some who have children – seems what
    happens to them – they care not a jot.
And if they take responsibility at all – well, that just
    depends.

Most of what has caused children to,
    "go wrong" – is "absent parents" ...
"Train up a child in the way he/she, should go –
    and when they are old, he/she, will not depart
    from it ..."
In God's Word we're told ... not much chance
    to train when – each in a different place.
If you are training an animal – time is
    required together – even to learn to sit.

Only Truth

We each need search our hearts ... God does;
Pray and ask forgiveness ...
Nothing hidden from Him can be;
His All-Seeing Eyes do see.

We may fool others for a time;
God's never fooled at all ...
Best confess sin to God we find;
Or on Him not to call.

God is due ... and requires our best;
As He looks in each heart ...
Only His truths will stand the test;
Bible's ... the place to start.

Can't Change; Penalty Remains

The Ten Commandments are part of God's law,
Moses received them, yet, God he never saw;
Character is measured by God's rules,
Why, now provides this century's controversy's fuel.

Some make the laws from seeds they've sown,
It seems God's laws they think to have outgrown;
They need no help, "when well" from God at all,
Forgetting, God, anytime, their name can call.

What about the generations yet to be? ...
Generations set before so lax is what they see!
With the examples and teaching they get ...
Look what we've come to and end isn't yet!

Discipline in home and school is antiquated,
Our courts become the judge... so stated
Rules enforced are all but nil!
A spiritual "moral gap" they cannot fill.

"Train up a child in the way he should go;
When he is old, he will not depart from it;"
That's God's way, He isn't our foe ...
We're God's creation; instead of Him many choose woe.

God so loved the world, He sent Christ to die,
Many refuse and salvation try to buy,
Christ died on the cross that we might be saved.
He shed His blood, and life freely gave.

Why should man exalt himself?
In love, God gave His only begotten Son,
Without God, where would man be left?
The Redeemer will be a judge when life is done.

Who is man that thou art mindful of him?
Though exalted on high, seeing evil's trend.
God's love extends in Salvation to each one;
For this, Lord, You sacrificed Your own Son.

There are those who declare a new set of rules
That's what is needed, everywhere and in our schools,
When if it weren't for God's kindness and love,
All who oppose Him could be struck down
    from above.

Forfeiting Rights ... Squandering Opportunities

Be careful lest you forfeit your rights,
And squander your opportunities ...
God's Word gives requirements for bishops.
Adam and Eve were driven from Eden
Because of disobedience to God.
They plunged the human race "into sin,"
God forgives man, but does not restore
To the "innocence" man had before –
Man must pay the penalty of sin.
David took Bathsheba for himself
And her husband he sent to battle to be killed in war
God forgave him when he repented
But, God chastised with the baby's death.

God's Plan For a Long Life
(What are Yours?)

A foolish question to ask ... but, do you desire
and plan a long, abundant life –?
Would you like many, many years before the sound
or dirge of the fife? ...
You may plan ... choosing your own way –;
Yet, ultimately ... God's the ALL-knowing One ... He it is,
who has the final say.

Eph. 6:1-3, "Children, obey your parents in the
Lord, for this is right –;
Honor they father and mother, which is the first
commandment with promise – (of life) ...
That it may be well with thee, that thou mayest
live long on the earth ."
Whatever YOUR age – honor is due the father and
mother who loved and cared for you from birth.

Eph. 6:4 – has a direst message to fathers ... "Provoke
not your children to wrath;
But, bring them up in the nurture and in
admonition of the Lord" –
to follow God's chosen path ...
God's plan isn't always easiest at the moment ...
but, rest assuredly – it's ALWAYS best –;
We can read in the Bible, answers to life's quest ...
but, obeying is the ultimate test.

Honoring a God-fearing father and mother ... whether
you be old or young ...
Has its rewards ... knowing God's bidding you have
done.

In honoring parents, as God has decreed – it's honoring
Him in spirit and deed.
Accepting Christ as Saviour ... if obeying God's
commands, life is more abundantly lived – meeting
His demands.

Truth Prevails!

If not at first ... truth will prevail;
God's in control of all ...
All answer to God ... without fail;
As Judge, each name He'll call.

David prayed, God not let his enemies
Have triumph over him –;
More prayer we need down on our knees;
Victory is His ... don't ask when.

God always keeps His Word to us;
How do we answer Him ...
Do we obey without a fuss;
Or does our faith grow dim?

Christ came that we might have life;
And have it more abundantly ...
If we obey, there'll be less strife;
For all ... for you and me.

Failing to enjoy the life God gives;
Is truly our own fault ...
Troubles will come ... long as one lives;
Death, only, brings a halt.

So when we think, truth's pushed aside;
Not for long ... that is true ...
God being the Judge ... He will abide; truth prevail.
All wrong He will subdue.

If you don't have Christ as Saviour;
When death knocks at your door;
Suffering forever just begins;
Biblical truths ... not folklore

Can It Get Worse!

Many in our society are void of conscience ... so it seems;
The Bible says, "Conscience can become seared, as with a
    hot iron;"
A conscience ... can't be judged except by God's words ...
    as seen;
Man should follow God's plan ... the Bible warns.

Sodom and Gomorrah were destroyed because of sin ...
God destroyed them both by fire ...
Same sex relations ... more rampant there ... way
    back then.
As now, the conditions of long ago, were to man's
    existence dire.

Who would ever have thought Congress to be wasting
    our money,
Trying to decide ... what is considered a "marriage"...
God, in creation, placed Adam and Eve in the Garden
    that Adam tended.
A debate in Congress on "same sex marriage," by a
    few led.

Otherwise; they could not have fulfilled God's order –
    to multiply and fill the earth.
So long ago when the founding fathers planned our course,
No thought of "same sex marriage" or "abortion" came
    to mind.
Do you think ... Congress and the President would
    have tried to force, laws upon the people such as these
... to bind?

God's laws were considered the standard ...
Man has forever been plagued by sin –;
Things now debated ... trying to make into law never
    heard;
Each person will answer to God – many a sin to the
    Judgment deferred.

Understand or Understood?

Do you understand the problems facing
   others ...
Or do you try to forget – hiding your
   head in the sand?
Life is often just heartrending ...
   for your brother –;
Perhaps, a little understanding would
   ease the situation, as a helping hand.

Do you understand what it is to be
   misunderstood ...
To be classified as the culprit –
   when you've done the best you could.
Accused of deeds – you didn't do – nor
   indeed never would ...
Instead of wrongly ridiculing others,
   better trust God, and adhere to good.

Do your thoughts always dwell on being
   misunderstood? ...
Or do you spend time trying others to ...
   understand ...
Life will be more satisfying when
   we help others – as we should –;
Giving of ourselves to those in need –
   not for ourselves always first ... on demand.

There's power in prayer ... to help us –
   understand;
Not always be lamenting ... of just not being
   understood ...
Other's feelings are important, too – stretching
   all across the land –;
Everyone, at times, needs a little help – God would
   have us reach out, always doing good.

Why should others understand you and
   all your problems ...
When you have no concern – except for
   your own –
God expects us all to be our brother's
   keeper;
Helping as we can – when many times
   your heartaches are only known in prayer, at God's Throne.

Inside Out

Rot and hate are much alike;
From the inside working its might –
Most damage done to the hating one …
Just as rot inside is done.
Working its way … reaching out …
To destroy, whatever there is about;
Causing destruction wherever it can;
Through hate and rot – much misery to man;

Rot contaminates wherever it touches;
Hate eats upon itself… wherever it gushes.
Hate will destroy a life of productivity and love;
Vengeance is the Lord's; He will repay from above.
Leave off hate, which rots away at the spirit and heart;
Keep eyes focused on the Lord in faith – that's our part.
We need be busy serving the Lord, and working as we
    should.
With faith and love, to please our Saviour, we would
    worship with faith, as we should.

Consistency

Consistency is considered a virtue;
Stubbornness seems the same;
To distinguish between the two;
Is part of life's game.

When standing for that which is right;
Consistency ... is what's true ...
Confidence reaches so great a height;
Whether it be you or me.

Stubbornness, it's called, when one's wrong;
Not changing when you're shown;
If evidence's given clear and long,
Name ... consistency ... is gone.

Action

When trouble comes ... we want immediate
    action ...
Certainly, there are things, while praying –
    we can set about to do.
Many times, we see so little of the things
    that's caused our heart's contraction;
Things aren't always as they seem –
    nor how it looks to you ...

God sees the whole of the cause and
    entanglement ...
He knows all ... from inside
    out.
Even the wicked, with the devil on their side,
    on destruction bent ...
Don't have a chance to have their
    way when God in His wrath turns it about.

We must trust – obey and pray – the wicked
    will always have their say ...
God is so gracious, loving, understanding
    and good ...
One thing we can know ... the wicked
    with the devil – won't forever have their way,
We must contend in what's right ...
    God's Word teaches ... this is understood.

A Drought In and On the Land

Oh, the sun is hot ... so is the blowing
    sands ...
The grass looks all dried out – having to be
    watered well –;
All flowers and shrubs need extra care
    from the drought to defend.
All garden plants are withering in the hard
    ground where they stood ...

A drought ... so dry ... so hot ... so hard
    to endure;
Such a long spell of dry weather ... causing much
    "praying for rain."
God is the One who can remedy what is
    wrong – His judgment is pure –;
All the creation suffers when God withholds
    the rain – there's necessarily much pain.

Man's spirit also suffers from a drought
    of the soul of God's true teachings –;
Values cast aside ... that were paramount
    in building our great nation –.
Bible truths set forth in old-time Gospel
    preaching –
Cutting straight God's message ... not fearing or
    turning from the drought of the spiritual situation.

To Judge

Who are we to judge each other,
When we are overwhelmed with faults.
Setting our own standards – needs come to a halt.
God's Word is the basis for judging another ...;
But, to judge ourselves, and not to exalt ...
If we exalt ourselves – we are abased further;
When we examine ourselves – our spirits we nurture.
When critical of others – harsh judgment for ourselves is
    wrought.
Prayer can pull a life together as a suture ...;
Mending the rend made by sin thus caught.
Perhaps, we'll be reluctant to judge in the future;
It was "Christ" who died, and our Salvation bought!

Looking in the Mirror

We look into the mirror ... to show us how we
    appear ...;
We wash our face – comb our hair, and see if the
    part is straight –.
If we care to see on the inside – we read – the mirror –
    God's Holy Word – dear.
It's easy to sum up – by these standards
    how we really rate;
We may not be honest with others, but in
    our own hearts, we know a multitude of fears;
Displeasing to God, if we harbor any known sin –
    not confessing – up to date ...;

It's as if we look into the mirror ... then
    forget the look we take ...;
God's Word does convict – mirrors the inside
    filled with sin ... jealousy, envy or hate.
If we have for no reason – without legitimate
    cause – labeled a murderer, ... our fate.
We need review our look – in God's Book –
    asking forgiveness before it's – too late.
If we have wronged another – it's plain in
    God's Word – it's on our pate ...
Before the Lord will accept our gift on the
    altar, we must make things right – or no use
        to pray and wait ...!

The Bible teaches we cannot lay claim, to
    be walking in God's light – if hating our brother.
A person having such hate – needs look into
    God's mirror – to see sin's darkness ...
If we love our brother ... we do abide
    in God's light ...;

When hate so fills our life ... we walk
in the night.
Of great assurance to our hearts that we
know Christ – and do not lie ...;
Is when we love – keep His Word and
commandments – which are always right.

It Won't Matter

Sometimes, people choose to have a
    different standard … so as not to blame;
When judging actions of men and
    women – harsh judgment of women to refrain.
Each person is responsible – man or woman –
    little known or fame.
But, one thing we can all know – in
    God's judgment … all is fair – it will be the same.

Character is of utmost importance for
    one and all –;
When lies are told … and told again –
    so many views – they do appall …
Racking one's brain to know just what's …
    to remember … or convenient to recall;
Lie upon lie … twisted to a turn – will
    be a liability – tasting of gall.

The truth never in the telling … does change
    the way it's told;
Nothing to try and remember in truth – but, telling
    more lies – a hundredfold –;
If those who habitually lie – could only see
    the way they appear, being so bold …
"Wisdom is far above the price of rubies" –
    silence is, "gold!"

Poetic Forms

God's Gift to the World
(Quatrain)

So important was Jesus' birth;
He came to save you and me;
For God so loved, the world He gave,
Christ came to set the lost world free.

Jesus' life on earth was perfect,
His miracles proved He was God's Son;
The multitudes did follow Him:
Many believed when He was done.

John, the Baptist, baptized Jesus,
An example to those who believe;
There's no saving power in water;
Salvation in Christ, be not deceived.

To bring salvation to the world,
He was crucified on the Cross,
It's a gift of God, and … not by works;
By grace through faith, He saves the lost.

The birth of Jesus blessed the world
On Calvary, He willingly died;
In death, He obeyed the Father;
He shed His blood, all sin to hide.

Jesus' birth was important to the world,
Christ's death needed to pay sin's price;
His resurrection imperative for eternal life;
Where the soul of man never dies.

By accepting Christ, we are saved;
Salvation is to man, God's gift,
We'll live eternally in Heaven,
Christ, the first-fruits of them that slept.

So important was Jesus' birth,
He came to save you and me;
For God so loved the world He gave;
Christ died to set the lost world free.

.

We May Run, But, We Can't Hide
(Quatrain)

Whoso rewardeth evil for good –
Evil shall not depart from his house:
Though exalting himself as he would,

Yet, showing self not as a man, but a louse;
An evil man will seek rebellion ...
A cruel messenger shall be sent to him.

He that justifieth the wicked ...
And he that condemneth the just, both
Are an abomination to the Lord.

A wicked doer gives heed to false lips
And a liar giveth ear to a naughty tongue.
Heart overflows with evil as honeycomb drips.

Furnace and refining pots for silver
And gold, but, the Lord trieth the hearts.
Searching out all evil ... where the heart rots.

Whoso rewardeth evil for good,
Evil shall not depart from his house:
Exalt self as he would – matters not ...
    comeuppance!

I'm Glad to Be Me
(Terza rima) - from 13th century.

When you think everything is going wrong,
And begin to feel sorry for yourself
If you really look, you'll know before long;

There's no one in this world, trouble-free left,
The Bible says, "Man born of woman is ...
Few days and full of trouble" ... none bereft;

This includes everyone ... the whole universe:
If you had others' troubles not your own;
Complaining might be left out of life's verse,

With self-pity discarded, cut to the bone,
The hardships endured would seem rather small;
Not wrapped in self-pity ... but, standing alone.

With faith in the Lord, upon Him we call;
Leaving burdens at the foot of the Cross;
Life can be lived as a long banquet hall.

Trials will come ... they separate the dross ...
That we might be more pleasing to the Lord;
Refusing to follow Him ... is our loss;

Losing blessings and Heavenly rewards;
The Lord chastens those who belong to Him,
God's Word is likened to a two-edged sword;

Thankfulness will help troubles to grow dim,
Counting blessings lift from despondency's pit
Life's cup is filled with good things, to the brim.

Christ came that we might have life and have it
More abundantly ...we're told in Holy Writ.

Reality is Different
(Sonnet)

Polite … quiet … adjusted … seemingly so;
Underneath such turmoil seething inside –;
Nothing falling in place in the dark space;
Though jumbled – vying – wanting what was not.
Past presses upon spirit's emotion …
Never vanquished while there's reality –
Faith gives light, which strengthens with devotion;
The mind does do turns at legality …
Not changing values – the same for all time;
Doing some sorting – putting all in place;
When true to self – paths easily defined –
To God, allegiance is due, in the race;
As loving as true self-worth lies underneath;
Truth – the base for character – will bequeath!

Looking Down Memory Lane
(Sonnet)

Looking down memory lane where I have passed,
Standing on time's indent – though looking back.
Much escaped the light and dark shadows cast,
Path lies straight ... much ... now travel doesn't lack.
Obscured but much protection can be seen.
Eyes not deterred from goal, as summit seized.
Obstacles not deemed, as none to see.
Meandering through, as wind with leaves, do tease.
Decisions after many a life's path,
Trust in the Lord overcomes much danger,
Faith sails unhampered o'er boulders and ravines,
Though to troubles, never being stranger,
Faith sees the best route to take,
God did lead and provided what was needed.

Waiting
(Sonnet)

Sometimes, we wait for something good,
At times, we wait – when never we should.
Anxiety, in the waiting ... nerves on end,
But, praying – a good message to the nerve system sends.
All anxiety and with problems surrounded,
But, always in the past, God's love ... abounded.
Though we are weak and unsettled,
His strength is stronger than all metal.
Though His power is always available,
And God, the only One infallible and salvageable;
Still, the choice is Christ, a personal one;
You must repent and accept God's only begotten Son,
Then waiting takes a different turn,
We wait on God – in His time we learn,

.

Serenely – Waiting or Anxiously?
(Sonnet)

Sometimes – we wait ... it's all we could;
At times, we wait ... when never we should –.
Anxiety – in waiting ... nerves jangled on end;
But, praying – a good message, to the nervous system send;
All anxious and with heartrending problems ... surrounded,
But, remembering in the past – God's love abounded –;
Though we be weak ... and unsettled ...;
His strength is stronger than all metal.
Through Christ, God's power is always available;
And He is the only one ... infallible –.
Still, you must choose – the choice is a personal one;
You must repent – and accept God's only begotten Son.
Then waiting ... takes a different turn –;
We wait on God – in His time – the tables He'll turn!

More or Less
(Sonnet)

To write a sonnet,
Why worry so ...
Just put it down –
As those of renown.
Some lines are short;
Some are written long.
So uneven ... they wont to be;
Syllables so numbered;
Five, seven, eight or three,
Even lives not numbered the same
So as long a story told – some fourteen!
I'll just ... finish my lines serene;
A rhyming scheme ... why does it matter to me?
A type of Sonnet – combining all there be!

Jesus Said, "Suffer the Little Children to Come Unto Me" (Matt. 18:5) (Triolet)

And whoso one such little child receives,
Jesus recognized it as done unto Him:
The evil done as well as the good ... He Sees!
And whoso one such little child receives ...
Then "abortion" is as unto Him ... logic agrees:
At the Judgment, He will look upon and condemn:
And whoso one such little child receives,
Jesus recognizes it as done unto Him.
.

Our God is the God!
(Psalms 139:15-16 and Jeremiah 1:5)
(Triolet)

In Thy book all my members were written:
Let God be true and every man a liar!
Curiously wrought in the lowest part of the earth;
In Thy book, all my members were written:
Fashioned ... when as yet there was none of them;
Though unborn ... Thine eyes saw my substance ... prior;
In Thy book all my members were written:
Let God be true and every man a liar!

.

If You Must Brag
(Triolet)

If you must brag, let it be on the Lord.
The Bible tells us, let another praise thee, not thyself.
The Lord will give to each his own reward.
If you must brag, let it be on the Lord.
The Bible's likened to a two-edged sword,
Our praises should all be to others left.
If you must brag, let it be on the Lord,
The Bible tells us, let another praise thee, not thyself.

Haiku

no smile
eyes dancing with light
secret's known

Haiku

rosebush
perfumes the trees
no hybrid

Haiku

cool breeze
sun sets beyond mountain
hammock

Haiku

to think
need think, think
still think

Haiku

so quiet
with eyes a sparkle
can't deceive

Haiku

false words
the eyes resist
tell

Haiku

blackout
actions with words
won't tell

Senryu

self-pity
is always wasted

Haiku

come see ...
diamonds overlay the grass after
a rain

Lilacs
(Cinquain)

Lilacs
In the morning
Fragrant dripping with dew
Seems yesterday we parted ... when
You died.

More on Lilacs
(Cinquain)

Lilacs
Purple and white,
Fragrant, spiked flowers;
Nostalgia accompanies down through
The years.

Haiku

lilacs
are an old flower
with fragrant spiked blossoms

Lilacs, an Old Flower
(Cinquain)

Often,
In the morning;
Fragrant, dripping with dew ...
Bring old memories to life; they can't ...
Bring you.

Senryu

wrappings wet
with tape falling
apart

Senryu

he might make delivery
if memory's good

Senryu

the ink
had already run
together

Senryu

what solutions
there'll be to the
problem

Senryu

on he goes down the road
hope he remembers

Haiku

the sun's
rays are shining
again

Haiku

a fine rain is
still falling
down

Haiku

soft wind
still blowing the air
much cooler

Haiku

spring showers
brighten everything
in sight

True Values

Family values ... we hear so much about ...,
One family may value one thing – another, some other –;
What's morally right ... should they all have, without doubt;
The Bible's the basis and objective – search no further.

Mastery By Faith
(Cinquain)

God's love
Leads ... Love with faith
Needs follow; the more trust ...
Less concern, and doubts ... are vanquished.
In praise.

Haiku

what's in sight
looking back, forward or around
you choose

A FOOTNOTE About the RENGA Poetic Form

Renga originated in Japan; both haiku and senryu come from renga. Each stanza links to the one before it, but not to the one before that. Writing renga originated as a party game or contest, where poets gathered and wrote poems together, called "tanka." They could be 1,000 or more stanzas, but 100 stanzas was the usual length back then. Renga of 36 stanzas is the popular form in today's times, like those written by Maxine!

For Viewing
(Renga)

lake viewed
from patio looks
so calm

lily pads are taking
more space

frogs like
to play games where
they float

a cool place where fish
seek shade

fishermen
know just where
to cast

old stumps are favorite
hiding places

beavers
build their own place
to hide

cutting trees they work
on their home

there used
to be a weeping
willow

along the brook that winds
the forest at ease

soft wind
ripples as sun dances
on water

tall grass sways in
the breeze

while bugs
struggle up the
long stems

all kinds of insects heard
in the trees

tree frogs
and katydids sing
their song

wind whistles singing in
tall pines

barking
dogs heard hunting, but not
intrusive

solitude only interrupted
by people

no more does it sweep water
of the lake

deer come
to drink on the
far side

bright flowers grow along
the bank

berry vines
reaching out to trail

God created everything
with order

man has
interfered since the
beginning

choosing to disobey in the
garden of Eden

rebelling
is the nature
of man

a detour to the blessing's
of God

walking
in woods where it's quiet
a nap

always
hurry to get there to
go where

man is a slave to the clock
and time

hands that
always push one
along

to eat, go to work, eat again
then to sleep

nature
has its own
schedule

awake and it's dark but dog waited
to lead the way

the moon
and stars are shining
brightly

looking forward to more spring days
the Lord has made

When the Snow Melts
(Renga)

winter's
dark cloak can't
cover all

strong winds
carry autumn leaves
across the yard

snowfall makes the ugly
shine with beauty

fallen rose petals
cover the grass

soft snow
icicles glistening
on trees

turning brown
during the season
for rest

children make snowballs
to start a fight

dull colors except
the green trees

cheeks red
with the cold
they laugh

the cedars
continue green
all season

losing caps and mittens
but having fun

a bird sanctuary
with berries

going inside
hot chocolate and laughter
fire crackles

bird houses
so confusing
too small

dog ambles out alone with
coat and no leash

shelter with lots of room
then rest on top

red bird
in tree top resembles
ornament

beautiful contrasting colors
red and green

lots of green
throughout God's creation
some red

red in sky of blue with
fluffy white clouds

red sunset
gives viewers much
pleasure

rest the eyes by looking
at horizon

to play
with the children
is fun

after winter they'll all
be outside

his turn
to take the air
and freeze

he's so cold he needs
to run a race

the rabbit
he sees only hops then hides
isn't fair

he's heard say, "Life's like
a bowl of cherries"

anyone knows
there has to be
the pits

it seems there's more pits
than cherries

school days
he watches the street
caring for them

in his "mind's eye" he can
see only green

grass growing
so fast everyone will be
in the yard

not much work going on, but all
he'll have to do is watch

it hurts
to lead a dog's life
when a pet

later he'll watch hummingbirds
light on flowers red

Poetry

When reading poems of yesteryear, stop and think,
    Life's dire link
The world's best poetry is in the Bible…
    God's Word needs be heard.
Desiring to hold the past in arms that list,
    Need resist
Poetry in the Bible is plain to be read
    His Word spread;
God calls plainly for man to return to Him;
    Though faith's dim
All people will answer concerning His Christ,
    God's not biased.

To think on God's Truths which last forevermore;
    Spirit's soar …
When God's Word falls on receptive eager ears;
    Then one hears –
God calls for repentance and faith to be saved;
    Man's depraved;
Let me write in humility and write … plain, though
    Oft writing Sin hath stained.
Salvation God's grief through Christ His only Son …
    … Only One –;
Christ died on Calvary's Cross for your sin and mine
    … Love … defined.

Thought

Pondering

Who's Your Friend?

Is a friend always the one who smiles, with a pat on the
    back – no matter what? …
Or is a friend the one, even if you don't like it – will
    tell you what's what and what's not?
With the one who truly cares about my
    well-being … so where I'll always cast my lot.
If the smiling, "so-called, friend" is all you've
    got – when storm clouds gather – they disappear –
    they care not a jot!

Just For Me!!!

What I desire is what should be...
Everyone should have no trouble to see;
That I'm what's important ... at least to Me;
Others count so much less – that's MY decree.

No matter if sickness is a great part;
As long as it isn't ME ... doesn't have heart;
Though the one disabled needs rest ... to start;
Won't bother me ... I'll just put horse behind the cart.

I'll have my way in all that I can ...
As I look around ... everywhere to scan;
What's best for ME ... being my own fan;
Should be to others as to me – nothing but GRAND.

It's being self-centered ... others do say;
Not caring for family ... night or day ...;
Selfishness is to Me the only way;
Living for SELF ... not withholding MY pay.

Forgetfulness

Forgetfulness seems to be rampant ... reaching
   the old as well as the young;
We say we must remember ... it seems
   we only remember to forget ...
Thoughts drifting in all directions –
   minds play hide and seek, as clouds drift among;
Trying to remember – in May as well as December,
   feeling responsible – in owing ourselves a debt.

Helping to remember by
   a string around one's finger –
Seems so obsolete ... when passing from
   May to December –;
You never remember where
   you put the ball of string – and that's a hindrance ...
Your hands are stiff and sore, can't tie a
   knot anymore ... no longer limber.

Forgetfulness plagues us all ... but, let
   us – even if we don't remember –
     never forget;
God expects repentance ... for our sins
   and shortcomings ...;
Then He is the One who forgets ... not holding
   them against us – serve Him and not to fret;
Prayer and trust in the Lord is the answer to much –
   forgetfulness – with truth it rings.

Why?

Why not tell me ... if what I hear is true,
Why do you hesitate ... tell me – tell me – do.
Why be afraid ... of tales that are told –;
Why do you think ... one would be so bold.
Why not speak up ... don't build a case against yourself –
Why not search out ... the hidden foe.

We are our worst enemy – at times it seems –
The devil looks about ... the best route he deems,
A person taking a stand against himself ...
Defeats his cause ... respectability bereft –
If another belittled ... treated you the same,
Temper would flare ... placing the blame.

A person needs respect others – also himself,
Can't respect others – if respect for self has already left.
When a thing is told ... which isn't right ...
To not make straight ... is not so very bright –,
Many lives suffer ... unnecessary pain –;
Because some are so stubborn – from repentance refrain.

Why build a case against yourself – never can gain,
Why not take stock ... of life that remains;
Why not take time to right ... what is not –;
Why go along with whatever – the devil's got.
Why not respect the one closest to you ...
Why don't you know ... it's you – you – you!

Window in Time

Getting just a glimpse through the window
   in time ...
Looking at just a small part, of the past
   with future in mind –;
All our thoughts ... and with each ...
   character to build or decrease –;
Lofty goals help to build ... perhaps to
   mold – though out of reach –.

A glimpse – looking back ... helps if taken
   in stride ...
History repeating itself ... lurks in the
   corner – yet, not outside –.
Ready to show forth – what has been –
   will ever be –
Prompted by human nature –
   residing in you and me.

If the window becomes clouded –
   blocking your view –.
Take a moment ... to think back –
   reminisce and review ...
All that has happened ... we can see
   clearer now –
Though the picture we see grows dimmer ...
   yet, brighter the understanding – as head we bow.

Someone Other!

There are people who spend their life wishing
    they were someone else;
This is a miserable way to go through life –
    even the body in bad health rebels.
Why not be thankful for the time God gives –
    make something of yourself ...;
Help another in the process – something of
    yourself – give back as you live ...;
We have no decision as to the family or nationality
    of which we are a part;
But, it's our life – where begins our responsibility –
    that's where we start.

We have no choice as to how we are born –
    rich or poor ...;
We need be careful we never disgrace the
    name we share – the one our parents' bore.
Whatever our race or heritage ... consider
    with all due respect;
What heartaches and troubles our forefathers ...
    came through – not able to deflect.
For to be where you are now ... many
    have paid a price ...;
The opportunities you now enjoy ...
    paid for long ago – yea, more than thrice!

If you ever feel ashamed ... of your own
    nationality or race;
Put yourself in their place ... life without all
    the modern advantages laced.
Perhaps, your plight would be much
    worse ...;

You might have just given up – withered under
    their pressure – you wouldn't be the first!
No shame in an upright life ... though, perhaps
    poor;
Not expecting a handout – working to keep the "wolf"
    from the door!

Moral values if taught while you are malleable
    and young;
With the teachings of Christ – as a protection
    between you and the world – hung ...;
Knowing Christ as Saviour – your life will be
    woven in a strong pattern;
With the light of Christ shining through ... as
    a beacon or lantern.
So ... it matters not – what your race be – or color;
Christ looks on the heart ... the same.

Envy

The Bible says, "Who can stand before …
    envy?" …
And, "Jealousy is as cruel as the grave" … it's
    manifest penalty –;
If what a certain person has or does always
    seems better to you than any …:
Why not take stock … see what values
    they possess … the envy of many!

Envy ruins many lives … always envious
    of one person or another –;
What's wrong with things your own … not
    always desiring the other …
You need make a better choice if you
    are prone to think someone else chooses better.
Be your own person … not habitually to be
    to someone else a debtor.

Best not to marry, than always think some other's
    spouse was a better catch for you …
Being satisfied or appreciating what we have …
    there are so few –;
If we ever take time to think … perhaps, we
    our own lives need review …
Try doing right … getting priorities in sight –
    improving on self in lieu –!

Set Watch: Some Do - Others Could!

He who doesn't work ... doesn't eat!
God's Word is plain and always right:
"No work," does of laziness reek?

Many flee work like a bird in flight;
Just ignore it ... or misconstrue! ...
As it comes near, it gives great fright.

Enjoyment comes when work pursued,
With spirit of God's Word to lead;
With hearts in thankfulness renewed.

One's work can bring enjoyment free;
Another of God's many truths ...
Side-swiped when false to truth careens.

Some won't work ... laziness in lieu;
While others bask in life's blessings ...
By working, learning something new.

Not used abilities, take wing ...
Talents when used are much improved;
Attitude right ... from cooking, to one who sings!

Work of the hands gives joy or feud,
Only difference in work and play
Within one's heart, is how it's viewed.

Liking one's work certainly brings joy to stay!
A blessing of God that isn't new ...
Some enjoy life, while others nerves are frayed.

Work takes hold ... holds boredom at bay,
With enjoyment of what we do!
Either add joy to life or serpent's sting.
Tally kept in heart ... if it's joy or feud.

My Way!

My way has to be right ... that's just the
    way it is –
What I said? "Yes, I'm positive – though
    really don't know for sure," ...
Yet, explaining the way it is ... my way
    certainly ... not his!
That's the way it has to be ... simply
    because no other way will do for me –.

My way of things is always to be in the –
    limelight ...;
It may not be the way it ought or
    should –;
Doesn't matter if it makes sense ...
    it just might ...
It isn't important what is best or right –
    that's the way it is – or could be if it would.

Just a Glimpse

Looking back in time through the window
    afforded ...;
Seems at first – as seeing through the
    little end of a telescope –
Barely in view are things so near –
    seeing from afar.
As though come and go ... coming
    into focus – having no longer to grope.

The telescope of time has been turned about ...;
Clearly seeing the picture as on a
    big screen –;
Memory is a precious thing, but ...
    careful, or sometimes it takes a detour route –;
Pictures – in thinking brought to mind –
    are stored neatly – filling the screen.

At times, it's no doubt best ... some things are
    obscured – no picture to glean –;
Adjusting the telescope out of focus – the
    small end in place ...
Making all a puzzle – not following
    the scene –;
Serving as a protection for peace of mind – emotions
    all but erased.

One Among Many

Isn't there enough hurt ... without adding more?
Someone burdened down ... do you ignore?
Are you self-centered – and continue to think ...
You're the only one ... with wisdom to link –;
Others have troubles with heartache a plenty;
Each person is only ONE ... a number in many!

Never refuse to help or speak words of comfort ...
Careful in uttered harshness ... not unnecessarily curt;
Try to help those who continue to struggle –;
Their lives in disarray ... a terrible muddle.
Many in worse conditions than you're in ... to be found;
Trust in the Lord ... for a heart and mind that's sound.

After All is Said and Done

After the smoke is cleared – after the dust
   has settled ...
What is left ... is immense pain
   and hearts broken ...
It matters not to those who caused the turmoil
   and distress – hearts like metal
Is there regret ... is there repentance of
   the dastardly deed done – not a token.

Sometimes, you can't help but wonder ... why
   those causing such misery are left intact ...
Going on in their destructive way ... doing
   as they've always done – things their own way –
Running "rough shod" over all who happen
   to be on the same track –;
Stubbornness and rebellion can only run rampant
   as long God holds back.

Some seem to have no feeling at all as
   long as they themselves escape ...;
They have no real love for others – they're
   the only one ...
When life is ending ... getting a glimpse of
   life's setting sun ...
The Bible says, "after death then judgment ..."
   that means each and everyone – as the tree
     falleth so shall it lie – all has been said and done.

Common To All

You have troubles – heartaches and such –.
Aches and pains ... from head to heel?
One day you do better ... not hurting so much?
Circumstances play such a part ... in how you feel?

These things are prevalent ... common to man;
Yet, each surmises – when trouble arises –;
No one has ever suffered troubles, as now at hand;
Forgetting reality – how adversity comes to all – isn't the
    wisest.

The Bible says, "Man born of woman is few days and full
    of trouble,"
Also, ..."Man is born into trouble as sparks fly upward,"
Without the help of the Lord, man is broken rubble.
Heartaches, pain and trouble – from land to sea ...
    with every continent marred.

Going Ahead

Going ahead with life is sometimes
    difficult ...;
When it seems so many things go against –
    all dreams –;
Life isn't made up of fantasy, but reality –
    with much tumult.
The Lord gives peace in the midst – of trouble –
    though trouble comes in reams.

To go ahead – with living in a fruitful constructive
    manner ...
Takes courage and faith in the Lord –
    trusting in His all abundant grace –;
Joy in the heart shows, in a life and face as if –
    waving a banner ...
A helping hand, and a kind understanding heart –
    has lifted many from despair's dark base.

Never should one be too busy – or afflicted
    with unconcern ...
To ignore one in need of help – turning
    one's head as if just didn't see ...
The Lord said ... "When you have done it to the
    least of these my brethren, you have done it unto me –"
When we help others as we should – we'll be more
    the Christian we profess to be.

One never knows – can certainly never tell ...
The next causality to come, that may find you or me –;
God sees all – to Him we're accountable –
    no use to rebel ...
Our actions must need be chosen wisely –
    although to choose we're free.

Comfort

When all seems wrong –you just don't feel up to
    par ...
Headachy ... irritable, tired, discouraged and
    utterly exhausted –;
Wanting to hide out, nothing to mar ... keeping
    all humanity afar;
Hoping no one's knocking on the door ... as before,
    dragging you from your daybed.

Your favorite things ... rather threadbare, but
    only worn at home ...
House-shoes ... from many birthdays before ... now
    a hole in the toe –;
Yet, when they were gathered to throw away ...
    they were made to leave them alone;
Conspiracy to rid you of your valued belongings –
    with you unable to contend with a foe.

If just for today ... they would overlook ... and
    leave you alone ...;
Thinking on Heavenly things ... renewing spirit
    reigns supreme, life's mundane strife at bay;
Then tomorrow ... brings another workday, when
    again – you'll be gone.
Calling time-out ... just to slip away ... much more
    accomplished that way ... in another day.

What Might Have Been

Reminiscing as to what has gone before ...
    can take up all our time ...;
While what's going passed us, "now" –
    is where our life begins –;
The future is never here – the present
    swiftly passes we find ... then must look behind,
Wasted time in thinking back while life
    continues to spin and years descend.

When you think, "What might have been ..."
Look around you ... take note ... many are
    in a much worse, "boat," –;
God gave His Son on the cross that we
    might have salvation free ... no debtor;
Christ came that we might have life and have
    it more abundantly – to Him, our lives we need denote.

As time goes by ... catch it while you
    can ...;
Make the most of each day lived ...
    enjoying God's blessings as they descend;
Soon the time that's present now will be
    in the past, to scan;
Forever – in neglecting what time is, "now" we
    continue to say, "What might have been!"

121

So Much Trouble!

Seems life for me is full of trouble ...
That is right ... God's Word plainly tells us this is so.
"Man born of woman is few days and full of trouble,"
If you've read the scriptures ... you ought to know ...

Trouble is the lot of man ...
No use to be surprised, or forever complaining –;
We're made of the dust, but, God has His plan;
Obedience to God, through Christ ... blessings which
    overshadow life's troubles again and again.

Circumstances Cannot Confine Love

Doing the best with what she has
To provide for those in her care,
Trusting the Lord to see them through
With cupboard full, or be it bare.

Circumstances can't confine love,
It reaches beyond earth's limits,
Love such as this is from above,
And though a lifetime seems like minutes.

To save them heartaches is desired,
As they travel life's stony path ...
Weary travelers grow weak and tired,
Love of the Lord shields them from wrath.

Children are only on loan from God,
Parents answer to Him, someday,
Old-fashioned parents are not "mod,"
What a price some parents do pay.

When small, they learned John 3:16
They learned it when first they could talk,
No use waiting 'till in their teens,
The Lord leads in right paths to walk.

The years will pass and faith increase,
When taught at first what's important,
Faith, will not make troubles cease,
But, the Lord will help, when others can't.

Seasonal & Occasional

Thanksgiving Dinner, 1996

Our Thanksgiving food was so good ...
Mother's old recipe –
Chicken ... dumplings, tasted as it should;
With rolls, butter, iced tea.

Giblet gravy, dressing with sage;
Sweet potatoes, green beans ...
Cranberries ... appetite to engage;
Turnips cooked right ... with seasoned greens.

Rhubarb, pumpkin pie ... can't deny ...
With pecans and whipped cream –;
Thanks to the Lord our hearts do cry;
From whom ALL blessings stream.

If our lives would prove as much blessed;
As in years gone before ...
There'd be nothing to ask the rest –
Blessed of God so ... who needs more?

Holiday Time

When it's holiday time ... everyone expects
   excitement and lots of fun ...;
Much planning and work starts early
   with much to be done –;
Late into the night ... starting from
   early morn ...
Cooking, baking rearranging, decorating – much
   hustle and bustle is the norm –.

It seems there's a holiday for all but
   the women ...
The men and children go about their
   chosen pastime ... no limits ... set to when ...;
All meals to be planned ... preparation's
   complicated and grand –;
The women of the family ... all duties
   performed – working together as a band!

There should be at least one, "holiday" that
   really is such ...
Christmas, Thanksgiving, Easter – anniversaries,
   then family birthdays – there's much ...;
For the women in the home – holiday or not – work
   goes on ... and on ... and on ...;
"Holidays" ... as they're called – make for work
   and more work ... 'till we're thankful when they're gone.

Women who prepare festive affairs for
   family and friends – holiday here – holiday there ...;
Are a special people ... going to much
   extra work and expense ...
Not stinting with time, energy, resources
   or substance...;

But, where are the others – when it's
   turn about – taking their turn would life enhance.

There are some who … it seems to be –
   to serve and please –
When it's time to change about … turn takers
   … scarce and hard to find …
All should have the, "Holiday Spirit …" and
   "love." ALL hearts should entwine –;
Not just the few … who work and prepare,
   while some do nothing but complain and dine.

One Day's Enough

Again, it's time for "Father's Day!"
Only one day a year to note ...
More than one day? ... the answer, "Nay!"

Executive or one who works in hay ...
Love ... children to him should devote;
Again, it's time for, "Father's Day!"

More than one day ... spoil him it may!
So there's no need to take a vote ...
More than one day? ... the answer, "Nay!"

For Father's Day ... Mothers will pay!
Time in kitchen ... all in the same boat;
Again it's time for Father's day!

Cook foods ... where his desire does lay;
Preparing all foods on which he dotes ...
More than one day ? ... the answer, " Nay!"

Not much time for poems to devote,
In the kitchen, my time I'll stay.
Again, it's time for Father's Day
More than one day? ... The answer, "Nay!"

Happy Birthday

Happy birthday to you each day,
Every day the Lord giveth ...
"Our time," is His ... say what we may:
From time of birth to the last breath.

Each day is a day the Lord hath made,
Deeds stem from thoughts we have within,
Written in ink that will not fade
Until in repentance of sin.

Happy birthday, and many more.
May each day bring you joy and peace,
Love, happiness ... good things you adore
A faith in God makes all trouble cease.

Sufficient unto the days is
The evil thereof ... borrow none!
But, enjoy each day ... though it's His –
Presented to Him when day's done.

Happy birthday, ... now, don't forget
Each day is a celebration ...
Though many challenges are met:
Happy with Christ when life is done.

A Beautiful Picture

White snowflakes falling,
On green Cedar trees
The Cardinals and other birds,
Hopping around so free.
Red birds perch on snowy limbs.
Wind blowing mightily for all to see,
Vision hindered, lights seem dim.
Ruffling his feathers – rough as can be;
Off he flies.

The Love of Christmas

"Children" of all ages love Christmas;
From the gifts to the lights and gingerbread;
All the excitement – with such delight.
Can hardly wait until Christmas night.

In the midst of all the pleasures
Emphasis need be on the treasure ...
Christ, was the Jewel of Heaven,
Sent by God ... to save man from sin's leaven.

No Room in the Inn

The tiny Babe born in a manger
Came to die for the wayward stranger
He, who knew no sin – His life He gave;
Christmas celebrates Christ's birth ... but, He died
    our souls to save.

Snowshoes and Skates

Snowshoes and skates
Waiting outside ...
Snowdrifts piled high –;
Don't want to be late.

On Christmas morning
Snowshoes and sleds waiting outside ...
Show-drifts piled high,
That we view with pride ...
    where the rabbits hide.

The New Year

The first day of the Year has come;
Can't tell what will follow;
Trust in the Lord and you have won,
Then bell's ring won't ring hollow.

All deeds will stand the test of time;
Either for ... good or bad ...
Each to his account – yours and mine;
Rewards lost ... Oh! how sad.

The page is blank that does appear;
Another day in life ...
How time's spent should be without fear;
With trust and faith, not strife.

When we give answer for this year;
What will our answer be ...?
The reason is what to God is dear;
That's what counts ... you'll agree.

Spring

I love the spring,
When flowers bloom,
As falls soft rain.

When songbirds sing,
Notes fill the room;
I love the spring.

Girl wears the ring,
From chosen groom,
As falls soft rain.

With love on wing,
No room for gloom;
I love the spring.

The night will bring,
Dim silvery moon,
As falls soft rain.

Wedding bells ring,
Even at noon ...
I love the spring,
As falls soft rain.

Nature

Birds' Gossip

Did you ever take the time to listen in the quiet
    of day or night ...
To all the birds with their own ways of twittering
    with delight?
The owl says in such a soothing soft voice,
    "Who-who, who, ah, whoo!"
As the whipper-will answers – "Whipper will," over and
    over.
The Bob White answers, too, ... each bird its
    own music, does pursue.
While the Mockingbird has many voices – the
    interrupting is up to you.
The crows congregate at the cornfield –
    The "Caw-caw," symphony right on schedule,
Darting at any animal they see in sight – defending
    the territory they have chosen to rule.
God has blessed us with such a beautiful, interesting
    world.
Things of nature – the more we learn – the more
    unfurled.
We shouldn't in our enjoyment of what's given, forget
    the One who gave ...
Most of all, God gave His Son ... loving the world – you
and
    me, to save!

A Real Fisherman

A real fisherman ... whether he's fished
   in time, short or long –
Is one who has patience ... even when
   everything may go wrong ...
Line might break ... hooks be lost –
   bait soon gone –
In fact ... not discouraged ... when
   the day seems lost – ending with a song.

Much to gain besides ... fish for food –
   when hungry – there are sardines and crackers;
But, a day out by the lake – would be
   good for the all day "snackers"...
Easy to lose weight – when so busy
   casting – you forget to eat –;
When food intake is so cut down –
   "calorie counting" is already beat!

In other words, a real fisherman – would
   rather fish than eat –;
That in itself is an accomplished
   feat ...
So to lose weight and have some
   fun ...
Be interested in what you do ... that, above all
   else pursue – the scales will have a shorter run.

The nibbles and bits may come scarce
   and far between ...
But, if a fisherman's interested ... his eating
   will be light – appetite lean –
Yet, he'll look forward to catching his
   "work" up – and another day on the lake to spend.
Perhaps ... besides the peace and rest, he
   can bring a better catch in.

Quiet the Mind

Fishing is a soothing pastime ... quieting
    the nerves and healing of the mind ...
No matter if the fish are big or if ... not being "keepers,"
    are quite small –;
The results of relaxation are immense
    to mind and body we find;
Fishing does so much more for a person than
    the most extravagant trip to the mall.

It's the fishing that has the restful healing
    qualities ...
Not the size or number of the fish
    which are caught.
Since it's mostly ... just the fun of the
    fishing ...
For healing, and is insignificant, if the catch is big and
    many or no catch at all.

A day spent fishing in a beautiful
    placid steam or lake ...
Causes one's mind and heart to be
    revitalized by the beauty of the surroundings –;
Therefore, bring into focus the harmony
    in nature and of our God being so great.
Hearts are expanded with love ... seeing how
    love, even in creation, in so many ways has abounded.

Snow, is Snow, is Snow!

Snow ... each flake so unique – not
    one the same –;
Snow piling on top of snow – as new
    storms move in –;
Freezing temperatures continue ... with
    snow gaining in depth – still to remain;
All looks so pretty from the window
    beside the fireplace in the den.
The ones who must brave the snow
    and cold, need have our concern;
Daily responsibilities requiring exposure
    to the elements, which are often a danger;
Putting oneself in the place of those
    whose work leads to the ice and snow.

The Little Bud

The little rose bud,
So fragile – smelling so good;
Is the same flower that develops;
Beautiful, then losing all grace;
Petals wilting, drying – falling into space.
The same process works in the human race.

The little baby you see now, so cute –;
Will grow into the likes of you ...
Like the rosebud, in its prime,
And to see it wilting – seems such a crime;
The same will be with you and me;
Life is dear; we're only here – by God's grace.

.

The First Leaf

The first leaf ... coming from a little bud;
Tiny, green fragments unfolding as they would,
Each day with the sunshine, time and rain –;
The leaf unfurls ... in growth it gains ...;
There comes the time when with it, combined
    there are leaves covering all limbs ... each defined.
All leaves combined creating a beautiful leafed out tree ...
And a wonderful shade, by day.

Nostalgia
and
Romance

Growing Old Together

Once upon a time we were young – boy and girl;
Meeting by the Old Village stream seems a dream;
After some time, wedding bells for us did ring;
Many years have come and gone, but a short time it seems;
    In memory, they gleam.

After many years, our children numbered four;
From baby to grown-up, there were many chores;
Don't know how we'd have made it, if there'd been more,
One thing for sure, with life, we were never bored.
    All four we adored.

Love
(Sonnet)

When 'tis love ... only true hearts are aware of it;
No explanation ... to other mortals can be made.
All else blends into the mundane elements;
Other hearts excluded, not to the festivities bade.
A banquet of love ... hearts intertwined ...;
Yet, not complete without the other – timid, afraid,
Age-old thoughts of love – yet, new – do bind.
Made known to hearts ... not always old and staid.
Not only the young hearts – who search with tendrils of like kind;
Finding a heart – not following where space is ready and made,
Placing all the golden dreams dreamed, forever on a shelf
    defined,
In the keeping of a love – safe with moonbeams,
Restful and placid as a clear celestial filled sky,
Yet, all the anticipation of together – you and I.

Home and Family Life

Who's the Host, Who's the Guest?

If you weren't going to visit the ones
    you're planning to visit ...
Would it be just as agreeable for the
    ones you're to visit ... to come visit you?
Something to ponder upon ... what if they
    were the ones coming as guests ... several in number?
Would you have everything ready ... to welcome
    them as they, for you ... always do?

To visit or not to visit might be more thought
    upon ... if time was divided up ...
Each might just decide to spend their
    vacations, with own family alone;
Not depending upon someone else ...
    to see you relax ... with tea and cup;
Perhaps just staying where you are ...
    and vacation at home.

A Way of Life

A beautiful, happy child – born on a Sunday morn.
As flowers in spring or sunshine after the rain,
Or as a rainbow appears after the storm;
A joyous demeanor – mostly the same.
Beautiful and most special – true to form.
Life to her is fun – but, not a game.
No matter the circumstance – happy or forlorn;
Much ever the same, for excuses are lame!

Lending a helping hand to others is her view.
With her hand in God's hand, she takes her stand.
It sometimes seems there is only a few;
But, following Christ – life can be grand.
This kind of spirit – as refreshing as the dew,
A person needs draw a line in the sand.
Then there won't be so many mistakes to rue!
If all had the same values across the land!

Enjoying the blessings God is always giving;
That's as it should be – to be sure.
It makes for rejoicing and abundant living;
For mean spirits and sour dispositions, a sure cure.
Circumstances – not our values deciding!
What God allows, we can certainly endure.
Strength comes from knowing – God's love abiding;
Knowing we are His – stand for right and feel secure!

When a Child

When a child ... so many obstacles ... they
    seem to tall –
As we grow up – on the same we can look down ...
Where as before ... head up trying to see –
    so far from the ground –
A child's perspective is right for them –
    God expects adults – to listen for their call.

When a child – a house seems so very big
    though all but small ...
Security in love and care ... though
    bewildered much of the time –;
They'll not panic ... if at first their
    way they don't find.
Though they may get lost going from
    one room into the hall.

Going back to scenes remembered from
    long ago ...
All the things that were so overpowering
    are not magnificent at all –;
The huge rock over by the gate ... where
    for the bus, children used to wait ...
Now as an adult ... it isn't even great – since
    in size they've grown so.

Adults need to teach by example and
    deed ....
Children are due encouragement – protection
    and love – teaching them not to be afraid –;
So many fears ... adults to children –
    can comfort ... and be laid
At best ... grown-ups can't remember

everything when they were small – and every need.

A child is cheated …very much –
    so …
When an education is expected without
    learning about the Lord –;
The ideal time to instill what's right –
    teaching them the Bible, is a two-edged sword.
Getting through to them while opportunity
    awaits – discipline is a friend and not a foe.

Part of Your Heart

Each member of a family has a part ...
Their very own place in a loving heart –;
Feeling their pain ... discouragements that are sent;
Suffering with them ... your heart rent.
You hope and pray things will turn about
They'll turn to God ... blessings on route;
Meanwhile, you continue to be concerned
Waiting ... yet, hope while a lesson they learn.
Remembering when they were young and small;
Couldn't talk ... or even walk without a fall –;
While your heart continues to reach out
With love, you wait – desiring increased faith, not doubt.

All Home Together

Our two daughters are already here –;
The two sons are coming soon ...;
All four ... to us as parents are so dear;
Again for all to be here ... to each his room.
Their families will come, too;
With everyone joining in the fun –
Grandchildren ... only a few;
One granddaughter ... four grandsons.

Interesting to see how much they've grown;
Hear all the things they've said and done –;
We'll enjoy their visit ... soon they're gone ...'
But, while here ... such fun – not a quiet one among!
Blessings such as this ... from God do come ...;
A loving family is a special gift –;
They're not ours to belong ... only from God a loan;
With thankfulness to God ... perspectives shift.

For all
Of you!

He's Always Been There

The protector ... caring for us all – always understood;
More dependable in the bad times, than even in the good ...
When he's needed ... if at all possible he'll be there ...
Loving us so ... doesn't have to be told, emotions that are
    rare.

Remembering back ... so very many years ago ...
When we were both so young ... yet, loving him so –;
Still, down through time ... that love did grow ...;
And as older we grow ... learning better how love to
    bestow.

However, inadequate all words may be...;
It's the deeds that are done and actions you see;
God has given us time ... to learn and grow up –
As adults, God wants us to live full our "spiritual cup."

Calling him to preach, special to God ... special to me;
When God calls one to preach ... dear to God's heart ...
    he has to be ...
Our hearts are bound by an invisible cord so strong,
From my heart to his ... a love that belongs.

When God has finished with us here on earth ...;
After trying to fulfill ... a mission ... the earth the girth;
Together in Heaven ... we'll live for aye –;
Resting from years of trials here during our earthly stay.

At times, when looking for results of some work we've
    done ... they appear dim.
But, faithfulness is what God required ... with results
    left to Him.
If we continue to work, pray and live as we should ...

His blessings o'er shadow all hardships that we've with-
stood.

For: Carl

My Buddies

My buddies are really good friends!
Though members of my own home.
They are always doing – without keeping tabs,
Things to make life easier – they are prone.
No matter the hardships or troubles they've had,
They wait not until they're all gone,
To look after me, though weary to the bone ...
When, at them many stones are thrown.
I know – they know I love them so;
However dreary, things may go.
Thanking the Lord when life is low;
For ones so special facing the foe.
When they are about – wrong they will rout;
With God's help, if it's in their power to do.
It is, has always been, an easier life for me, they pursue.
As for me, I think of them – their lives in lieu!

The Magic Bush

A man had a notion ... he'd add to his
    rose garden ...;
Three special bushes – one for his wife –
    one each for the two daughters;
He'd get all three planted as a surprise and
    before the ground hardened ...
For the wife, a magenta called – "Angel Face,"
    but, for that he'd ask her pardon –.

A "Forty Niner " – red and yellow – a spectacular –
    for his older daughter –
The bush for the younger ... they didn't
    send the one he ordered ...
So – he'd, too have a surprise – he waited to
    see just what it would be –;
When it bloomed – the most beautiful and
    astounding bush of all – a multicolor or roses –
        his eyes were to see!

Too Much to Do?

So much to do ... some think it can't
    wait!
No matter the hours of planning, doing
    the best I can;
To have a schedule all worked ...;
    out;
Something much stewing and fretting
    about.
Planning so much, doesn't do much
    good!
Too many not working – interferes, can't
    do what I would.

Needing a little time ... slipping out of
    sight!
To get some much needed rest, which
    is my right.
Having my own dreams, the same as
    the rest.
Spending time with the Lord to be at
    my best.
There's just so many hours in a
    day
Some for work ... some for ...
    play!

.

Buy the Truth and Sell it Not

True preachers, long ago, endured much
　　strife –for oft the truth endangered their life;
They worked as did the Apostle Paul of
　　old ... the truth was never sold;
Without the big salaries, nice buildings,
　　and fine care of today, would preaching be as rife?
The gift and callings of God are without
　　repentance – not to put away and fold.

If God calls a man to preach ... he never
　　goes beyond God's reach;
No way to excuse ... the flimsy excuse of ...
　　turning back;
Whatever God says do ... His Word is
　　true – God will supply what's needed to preach;
God's grace is sufficient for our every need –
　　refusing to do God's Will shows what love
　　and faith we lack.

If there were no big salaries ... as of
　　long ago;
How many would lay claim to hearing God's
　　call to preach His Word and not to be denied;
A preacher shouldn't have to work, but, to
　　spread God's truth ... work shouldn't seem a foe;
On the souls of men ... there should never be
　　a price – Christ paid that on Calvary when He died.

A great preacher in days gone by told me,
　　of going on his preaching appointments;
He described himself as "Ichabod Crane:
　　riding his mule and as to how his clothes fit.
For awhile, he was in politics in Washington,

representing a great state – talk of his running for
  governor. ... among the gents.
He said after awhile he found preaching the truth and
  politics didn't go together one bit.

Knowing God had called him to preach His Word ...
  and so many who had never heard;
His life was spent preaching the truth,
  rescuing souls from Hell instead of in
  politics ... living well.
He's long gone to meet his Heavenly reward
  with his preaching, many hearts were stirred;
His call to preach he guarded well ... as have many
  others – knowing God's call to be the highest ... and
  not for sale.

Family

Remember the breaking of one broom straw? –
    so easily broken;
Keep adding another and another until you
    cannot break ...
'Tis the same with a devoted family –
    troubles only bring faith, a token.
One for all – all for one – whatever is
    needed – the provisions they made ...
Sorrow doesn't come to one ... it comes
    to all – allegiance golden –
One suffers not – without them all –
    passing through adversity's gate.

God is love – as a family He would have
    us loving as we should be,
Strength comes from God, as do all good things –
In times of great danger, one standing alone
    may be as a too lightly rooted tree ...
Facing a storm of wind – easily uprooted being
    only one – with no others, the roots easily fold.
A family bound by love is as a number of
    straws or a stand of trees.
With faith in God – standing together – not soon
    broken – with love to hold.

An Addition to the Family

A new baby … so much to do … much
   learning needed – but, just proceeded
So much diaper changing … formula
   mixing, too …
Baths are a necessary part of daily
   hygiene – needed.
All the things for a happy, healthy baby
   are eagerly pursued.

A few hugs and kisses – little arms
   reaching out.
Give much more back –
   than was given in their case –
To be lifted up and lovingly tossed about …;
The laughter and little voice crying for
   joy – almost more than a loving heart can bear.

So thankful to God for His priceless
   blessing …
Adding to the home such an anchor
   of love –;
Making hearts once centered on self –
   more pliable and mellow…;
Causing minds to be turned to thoughts
   of God Above.

A child is no less precious – as older
   they grow …;
To a true parent … they'll grow even
   more dear –
As your realize – troubles in life – will be
   a part of them – through which you before did go.
Strength for what lies ahead comes from

faith in God – Who brooks no fear.

Training a little one from the start –
    in the ways of the Lord …
Is the best legacy that can ever be
    given …;
Teaching values gleaned from His Holy
    Word –;
Will strengthen a life and by example show – God's
    way, is the way for abundant living.

Birthday Wishes

Happy birthday wishes;
May the day be happy;
For the birthday feast – many favorite dishes.
From start and to finish, may the day be "snappy."

Thankfulness to the Lord, constitutes a great part;
Thinking on all the blessings – over the past year;
Not only to me – but, those near my heart.
As years pass by … wishes very dear – many hearts say;

Birthday wishes … Happy birthday
May all those close – celebrate, too;
Enjoying the festivities … of the special day;
May all good wishes – with God's help come true.

Rest When You Can

After the holiday is past ...
With company come and gone –
Decorations put away at last;
When everyone's left for home.

Rooms put back in order ... once more;
Ready for summertime ...
They'll all be coming as before;
Not like this ... more sublime.

The excitement's not like Christmas;
Wait for them to come ...
Preparation's made – but, with much less fuss;
All ready to have fun.

Picnics and fishing ... a great part;
Each busy ... having fun ...
Need to rest before summer starts;
For when they come ... there'll be none!

Happy Birthday To Me

Happy birthday to me –
If that sounds odd ...;
... So let it be ...
We're all of the sod.

Thankful for another birthday to see.
So many blessings given of God;
Through Christ, His Son, I am set free.
I pray to always stay close to Him – ...

And to His chastening rod.
Through my Saviour I am redeemed;
Happy birthday to me...
Crazy? "No," sincerely and I'm, not "mad!"

Years Can Make a Difference

Can't walk, can't talk, can't feed self either;
Toothless, helpless, depends on another
For everything ... diapers to teethers.

If giving care ... most prefer a baby,
Loving and hugging to see it smile.
Most of the hard hearts a baby can stir.

When parents grow old in years and miles,
They need love and care as the young do;
Their life each day can become a sore trial.

Not able to do for those they love;
Nor can do for the themselves very well ...
Each day, trust the Lord's mercy above.

Where's the children who adored you so?
Some remember ... yet, many forget ...
To some ... growing old has made you a foe;

Unless, of course, there's a big estate,
And there's much substance in the offing,
With eye on, "main chance" of inheritance.

Just being old doesn't make for a dunce,
Senility ... isn't always the thing.

Will Your Family Circle Be Complete?

Loved ones gone before, are waiting there;
Those who have reached that Heavenly shore:
Escorted by Heaven's Angels fair ...
To bask in God's sunlight, evermore.

Some have been waiting for many a year,
To hear the trumpet sound, "time no more!"
The living know they shall die ... death draws near;
You choose ... not after death, but, before!

For God so loved ... He gave His own Son,
Christ died for ALL upon Calvary's Cross;
His blood was shed ... Salvation won,
Only faith in Christ will save souls lost.

Won't you prepare while your loved ones wait;
Making your calling and election sure ...
Accept their Christ, before it's too late;
Recall their teachings ... that still endure.

Are there those your still must witness to?
So Heaven's circle can be complete ...
The Master's bidding we need pursue;
In faith ... for doubting will bring defeat.

Loved ones gone before are waiting there;
Those who have reached that Heavenly shore:
Escorted by Heaven's Angels fair ...
To be with Jesus ... forevermore.

It's a Girl!

On the car phone – "Mother, it's a girl! You can
    bring the baby girl's clothes out!"
He called as soon as he knew … that's what
    it was about.
Anyone would have thought, the baby was
    already here …
Such excitement, in his voice … one could
    easily hear …
They had just come from the doctor's office,
    when he called me;
Just checking … both mother and baby –
    were as they should be;
Everything was alright – just to let us know,
    praying to God they remain so.
Hurrying to call as soon as he could …
    wanting everyone to know!

He said he'd like a little boy from the …
    start;
But, when the doctor, the picture did show –
    the little girl stole his heart.
So excited was he – counting a privilege –
    the tiny baby to see.
The doctor made comment – how she liked the
    camera – dancing and turning so free!
Months – going slowly – yet, to wait – until
    her time to arrive;
Already, she has the love … she'll have –
    it'll always survive!
Her daddy's excited voice … she'll always
    be glad to hear;
So filled with love – and thankful to God –
    before she even gets here!

Our First Granddaughter

(First little granddaughter) came for a
   visit ... only a few months old ...
She traveled a long distance with her Mother and Daddy
   her grandparents to see –;
We just knew she knew us ... heart to
   heart ... love at first sight – did it.
There'll no doubt be other grandchildren
   as before ... our little darling she'll
     always be.

Growing Old

Growing old ... older, year after year –;
So many changes ... then, I can't hear.
When I get up, it's hard to walk,
Can't just sit around – and talk.
Need exercise ... it's hard to get
What can I do, but sit and fret.

Growing old is hard to bear ...
Remembering when – to go here and there.
When time to eat ... nothing is sweet;
That's my favorite thing and hard to bear.
Everything I like – seems is off my diet;
Must watch out – cholesterol to fight.

Feeble steps – hands that won't work;
Around the edges – suspicion lurks;
Things I should have taken care;
To grow old is not so rare ...
But, many things I failed to do;
Many I shouldn't have done – quite a few.

... When younger you fail to see;
With health how careful you should be.
If you had only known back then;
You would live to the time you're in ...
Our body is the temple of God;
We need take care – we're only of the sod.

Growing Older

Have you noticed the pride in the ones' grown old –;
Self-esteem – comes from the inside –
   the way they think of themselves – works its way out;
Hanging as it were – by a strong, yet gossamer thread of
   the long ... long ago ...
So rich in memories – yet, caring what's going on around –
   trusting the Lord to direct their route.

The elderly – dress themselves – to look
   handsome, pretty and pert –;
Lipstick and rouge – new hair-dos, too.
   to some ... will always be a part;
If I live, to be older than I am – old
   age – can't be warded off – death is the alternative.
Meeting God, there'll be no escape – we
   all must die – returning to the dirt.

When you have opportunity and the privilege –
   from an elder to listen and learn –;
You look beyond the signs of age –
   to the eternal fountain of youth – that is the gauge;
As long as there's life ... while trusting our Saviour
   to lead ... His will not spurn ...
Though grief and heartache are always a part,
   faith in the Lord, all ills of humanity assuage.

Unconditional Love

Dedicated to Ho-Bo, Wired-haired, black and tan
Dachshund now 15 years old, and is still helping to do
books for Mother. He faithfully sits by my side each day I
type. We think he's the bestest and the mostest – all
twenty-two pounds of him. (pardon the slang!)
Although Mother didn't get to know Ho-Bo, this poem of
hers just "fits the bill, regarding this special little dog!"

No human being is ever so enthusiastic and
    eager for your return ...
As your own dog ... whether you've
    been gone an hour or day –;
It matters not if you are happy or
    forlorn – or many other things you soon learn;
A dog will all his loyalty and love
    not hesitate to display.

Many things we humans could learn –
    if only from our dogs to discern ...
For we never know – when we leave
    what the outcome will be –;
So when we fail to be happy concerning
    someone's return,
We need remember ... one isn't guaranteed an
    imminent return you see.

But, cherish the time God allows
    families to have;
Always be happy when one who has left
    returns again;
Many have left home with mishaps
    to hinder and follow ...
All the grand plans to be forever taken

out of hand.

Priorities need to be examined – things
   set in order –;
We can't take for granted ... fifteen minutes –
   for, of life God, is the Author;
When one returns ... knowing not if
   of life – just on the border;
We need learn to love and appreciate
   what, at times, is considered a bother.

Political

God's Laws and Judgments

Is our society, void of a conscience ... as many seem;
Conscience can become seared as with a hot iron;
Conscience ... can't be judged, except ... as seen by God's
    Word.
Many should follow God's plan ... the Bible warns.

Sodom and Gomorrah were places filled with sin.
God destroyed them both by fire, wrought destruction near
    and far.
Same sex relations existed way back then.
Conditions back then were rampant ... as now ... are dire.

Who would ever have thought Congress to be
    responsible ...
To decide what would be considered a marriage ...
God, in the beginning of creation ... placed Adam and Eve,
    in the garden to tend.
Same sex marriage ... trying God's plan to disparage ...

When the founding fathers set our course ...
Did laws on marriage or "abortions come to mind."
Years ago, wouldn't have been for Congress to force,
Laws upon man, contrary to what God binds – justification
    to find.

God's laws were considered the standard,
Though man has forever been plagued by sin ...
The things now debated ... as a law were never heard,
Sins each person will answer for – many to the
    judgment ... deferred.

Button - Button

Button ... Button ... who has got the
button – no one must peek ...
Just a game? ... Blind Man's Bluff? Tag?
"Who has got the Button? or Hide and Seek?
At the White House ... it seems anything
goes ...Congress has to turn up the heat!
The leaders our founding fathers envisioned
down through time were trust-worthy,
not weak.

Button ... Button ... the button is misplaced
forever lost ... one fears –;
Who did the firing in " Travel
Gate?" everyone is a demurer –;
Button ... Button ...who put the files –
in plain sight ... where they hadn't been for years?
No one knows who does the hiring ... or
the firing ... from all one hears.

Button ... Button ... where's the button or
FBI files – to many their privacy dear ...
Who hired this one or that ... perhaps, you shouldn't
ask – they may just jeer –
If one asks a question, which should be
available to all ... some may leer ...
It does seem the disillusionment of many,
perhaps, heretofore, hoodwinked.

Just Facts

So much we hear is our culture of ...
   today ...
"Don't sound so mean ... one shouldn't
   speak so harsh –;"
To speak what's true in modern times,
   just isn't the way.
One must hedge on the truth ... to fulfill
   the majority's wish.

When a preacher uses the Bible to preach
   what's true ...;
The congregation at the preacher may ...
   become miffed.
Even if he only reads ... what God says
   we're to do ...
God's Word isn't to entertain ... but, does
   condemn and uplift.

A politician who will state the unwavering
   facts ...;
Concerning his opponent ... over political
   barriers must leap.
There are many who choose tact ... no matter
   if the truth does lack –;
Civility may seem to smooth over ... where
   differences run deep.

Why not state the issues ... really lay them
   out ...;
If no difference in parties ... why not settle
   for anarchy???
Pretending ... shouldn't be what elections
   are all about –;
Hiding the differences in, "political ...

correctness": ... a lot of malarkey!

With those seeking office ... wouldn't it be
    nice ...;
If they were ABLE and CAPABLE ... their own
    speech to write –;
Hearing their thoughts and values ... not by
    a professional speech writer biased.
We need politicians who can write their own
    speech ... who will for right stand and fight.

The State of the Union

State of the Union … from whose point of
    view? –;
Perhaps, as many giving their view …
    as from many different angles …
Just as a photographer takes a picture …
    "shooting" what's in sight – taking a few;
Another comes along – identified subject – yet,
    the picture's all wrong – sometimes of a tangle.

State of the Union … is according it seems
    as to who's doing the talking –;
Someone else at fault – for all that's wrong –
    is what we expect to hear …
All sit and listen – seeming to hear – then the
    audience divided – takes the applauding;
Each division – not only by party – has its
    own agenda – with failing to fear.

What's the, "State of the Union?" … the Union that
    to all hearts – should be dear …
Divisions though many – there's never not
    any – still making the whole –;
A country – diversified – interests many – agreeing,
    disagreeing – working together to steer;
The best country on earth – God has richly blessed
    from birth – asking God to forgive and have mercy on
    our souls.

Opposing Ourselves

When we take a path ... opposite from what's
    right ...
We oppose ourselves ...when we walk
    the path ... with obscuring light ...
Time may go on for short or long ...
    will all catch up ... come day or night ...;
Much happier days if we travel unhampered
    by sin's weight ... basking in God's light.

What if a candidate running for office
    when going to the polls, opposed himself? ...;
Why was he in the race if ... he
    would vote for another – leaving himself bereft ...;
It would seem strange ... opposing
    himself ...at the polls.
When one goes against God – opposing himself –
    he loses out – taking the wrong route.

Expecting of Others

How can a person – when he has the advantage –
    expect of others. ...
What he already ... years gone by ... refused to do –;
Forsaking country – honor – a regiment of
    brothers;
Leaving the many to pursue –
    and the dead, not a few.

Now with orders – for masses ...
    to go –
When years before he was against –
    himself fighting – didn't mind saying so!
Privileged is he – Christmas is near – at the White House –
    Christmas tree aglow;
But, many have received orders to go ... at
    Christmastime in the cold and snow.

In times gone by ... the leaders would be the ones –
    ready to go –;
Rushing to the front in battle ... forever leading
    the way ...
Remember the time, David, the king – stayed behind –
    ignoring the foe –;
Troubles he had not taking the lead –
    when there was a need – at home he did stay!

Life is important and dear ... having his fears;
Each person's life is ... precious to
    loved ones as well as him –;
Peacekeepers? ... where war has raged for hundreds
    of years.

Sending our soldiers ... into the midst – with
  violence and hate up to the brim.

Many have families – small children ... dependents
  at home ...
Yet, going again and again ... to police the whole world;
Though our country isn't at war ...
  yet, many soldiers going and going and gone;
Why not those of the media and leaders so eager to
  send – take lead – let the dangers at them be hurled.

Policy would change – to conservative ... fast –
  we just protect the life – our own ...
Soldiers trained so well ... would get to rest a
  spell –;
Not traveling here and there ... the whole world to
  roam;
Not seeming to have a foreign policy ... all helter-
  skelter ... pell-mell!

Majority of Americans say, "No" ... they're going anyway
  – now what we must do is pray.
That God will keep them safe ... and make it a short
  stay ...
Let us all pray those responsible for sending them
  away –;
Be conscience stricken (if not seared) of their rash
  and brash judgment – everyday!

Judgment is coming – to one and all – with God being
  "Chief in Command" ...
No one in that day will push ahead –
  striving to be the head of the line;
With another's blood on one's conscience and
  hands;

According to God's Holy Word ... one will answer
in time.

Which

Did you ever play the shell game –?
Trying to guess which shell would make you
    the winner?
At the White House, no one wants to be named; ...
    therefore, no one will take the blame.
All that maneuvering that's done, but, to confuse
    and the truth to hinder.

Can you guess ... which shell the
    firing of the "travel office" is under?
Under which would you guess you'd find the FBI files?
They are all claiming ... it was just an innocent
    blunder – many there be who wonder –
If that is true – then of blunders, there's files
    and piles.

Under which shells is the recently questioned
    hiring of the security man?
He doesn't know ...and no one who did
    will take a stand –
It seems Congress will need increase its commitment
    to play the shell game ... yet – again.
The shells move by ... since
    The hand is quicker that the eye... catch me if you can.

Under which shell was the file for so long –
    that so suddenly reappeared? –
Upon a table in plain sight –
    as if by magic –;
For several years, this file disappeared –
    then showed itself as if ... something to be feared.
So much connected with these
    happenings – heartbreaking and tragic.

Eclectic

Just One

You may eat only one ...
Really shouldn't have any –;
After all's said and done,
Eating one or many ...
Being sick isn't fun –;
With allergies – refraining's ... the
    best remedy.

That Can't Be Me!

Noticed my clothes seemed to be shrinking each
    time they were laundered ...
After continuing for a time ... it came to mind –
    something other – was wrong –.
Had been so busy with this and that – hadn't
    taken time to see – whatever was wrong – was wrong
       with me.
One day, I stopped from rushing to and fro, and before
    a full-length mirror and took a good look and long –.

It wasn't my clothes ... a good look told me
    that – the weight slipped upon me pound by ounce ...
Needed to lose weight – not just a little ... there
    was so much fat;
Couldn't keep blaming shrinking of the laundry on
    clothes worn thin –;
It was I who had changed ... after so much washing – they
    were as they always had been.

Don't lay the blame – on the shrinking of your
    clothes –;
Take a look in the mirror ...step onto the
    repulsive – revealing scales ...
Just confess – it's the food, you "ET" ... and
    watch that weight staying on your toes –
Blame no one but yourself ... discard that
    fat – burning it off by exercise and diet – all else fails!

Style

Style – what is style – so confusing – what
    to wear – who tells you when and what ...
Does it always have to be ... something new –
    you have not ...?
Does one always ... have to follow with
    the invisible throngs ...?
Why not ...set a style – suiting you –
    your very own ...?
It's always monotonous ... with every thing
    the same ...!
Even in a voice – unchanging as the
    patter of the rain ...

Style ...? why not take a look 'round
    about ...;
Make use of the many things ... you
    almost threw out ...
From experience it has been many –
    times seen ...
Something at home – tucked away works
    better than spending – more green –
All dressed up in something new ...
    compliments expected ...??
What about – raves in the –"view" – of
    thing one time rejected ...?

Much time and money squandered – by
    all who have – in style alone invested ...
Good taste ... always in style ... classics
    are never bested ...
Some things called, "style" are no more
    than – a craze – a fleeting – fad ...

Such prices attached ... but, many don't
    realize until too late – they have been, "had"!
Be as the woman with a dozen children
    way back when ...;
When complaining, concerning –
    style – she thought to make her own ... was no sin!

Hot Lips

I bite my nails down to the quick ...;
Everyone around ... gets sick;
I've been threatened and I've been bribed,
I've said I'd quit ... but, lied –;
Red pepper ... for a finger dip?
Not to stop ... means hot lip!!!

Morning Monster

Looking in the mirror so fast ...;
Only hope ... dreams don't last;
Breath from a fiery dragons' den –;
Eyes all red ... hair on end;
I was the monster in my dream ...;
Really ... it's what I seem.

Me and I

I am I, I am me, I am always myself.
Everyone that's left can go sit on a shelf;
I am I – me am I – myself am I.
Must be something wrong with me, myself and I:
But, for the life of me – not one flaw I see,
Anyways I look – I just sigh – I wonder why?

Late or Not?

So many times ...we all hear,
Someone departed this life so dear;
As the late Mr. or Mrs. John Doe –;
Why the L-A-T-E whether – friend or foe?
Perhaps, "late" shouldn't be used at all ...
Could have been ... they were early to fall;

Many actions – not forsaken, but taken;
So – when we refer to one as late,
That means not keeping a certain date;
We don't know if they are late or not –;
They could have just left – on the dot.

Perhaps, best to say, "the departed ..."
Then someone will ask – where? – fainthearted
How can one determine – whether Heaven or Hell?
If one has Christ as Saviour – all is well –;
But, through neglect of accepting God's gift;
Thinking only of self ... trying to shift.

However, we are wont to speak the thing;
"Departing this life" – has a serious ring –
Being prepared to meet our Maker
Is what will count – can't be a faker
Then will matter not if early or late ...
One thing is sure – all will keep God's date.

The Big Test

Sleepy-head, sleepy-head, ACT time again!
… Have to get up … had to be shook …;
Need to hurry … can't be late –!
There's a certain time … just can't wait!
Where's my other shoe – one will never do!
Of course, I'll need my cap – a search I'll pursue.
Whew! Now that's done and finished …!
Oh, no! Seems my comb and keys have also vanished!

Here I go … made it at last –;
Where's my identification … need it fast.
Oh, they know me! It's my own school.
I know who I am – as a general rule!
But, this morning … you tell me …!
Feeling like this – I shouldn't have paid a fee.
Now, I'm here – no mistake – wide awake!
Ready to start! (no pencil) Oh, Lord, I pray a high score
                                    36 or 34
                              Help me make!!

When it's test time again … things will change!
Pencil, comb and keys – shoes and hat, I'll arrange!
Not stay up so late watching TV or a Friday night date.
… Getting up early … instead of late –!
I plan to get there … with time to spare;
All settled in place – not having to race.
… Studying hard can have its reward …;
I'll do my part … while asking the Lord.

A Counselor's Counselor

School has started again ... for the year ...;
A hectic atmosphere ... such commotion ... noise to hear;
Students rushing fast ... passing to class –;
Some needing schedules changed and fast.
Shortage of teachers ... makes scheduling rough;
With over-crowded classes ... leaving teachers in a huff.
The counselor has to know her job exceptionally well ...;
To balance all out ... getting ready for the bell.

Just as she thinks she has it all figured out –;
Any number comes ... needing schedules changed about.
While a teacher has only her classes to teach ...;
The counselor has to juggle ... reaching all gaps to breach.
She does a good job of a balancing act ...;
If she's able to get the classes everyone lacks.
If every teacher could be a counselor ... as the year does
        start;
No more criticism about counselors doing their part.

Doing what's best in the classes being offered;
Getting schedules arranged ... so they'll be right ...;
After this ...with the new year just begun –;
The counselor's job .. the gambit runs ...;
New students to register – classes already full, grade points
        to check;
Book work, report cards ... problems to solve to keep lives
        from being wrecked.
Though pushed for time ... she's the students' friend ...;
With love and concern ... she her help does lend.

Some parents, coming with children to register ...;
Note the harried counselor ... offering their prayers as a
        Christian gesture.

With faith in the Lord ... desiring their prayers ... she
    certainly does ...
To help her figure out what is ... isn't ... or was.
She must have the Lord to be a success ...;
Much of her work is confidential ... and not to confess.
Many whose work ... a counselor ... they chose to be ...;
Have found if they do their job ... there's little time free.

Many students are appreciative and comment on the help
    they get;
Those knowing the counselor goes beyond the call of duty
    ... yet –;
It's as if for them to see ... she holds a light ...;
Steering them right ... with in mind, education, not to
    blight.
Pointing to education – fairness they see in her as it should
    be;
Each important ... yet; to make their own decision, they're
    free.
Where she goes, students from years gone by ...;
Not only stop to talk ... but, frequently give her a hug ...
    they know why!

... In Life's Test,
Christ is the Answer

Springtime! And it's time for ACT Test ...
The time of year when it's hard to stay inside;
For one, it's more difficult than for the rest,
As a foreign exchange student ... here he resides.

His "host" country is waging war on his own ...
Where a Civil War has raged for hundreds of years;
Many ask why we're there and will not condone,
Concentrating on test's difficulties, midst his fears.

The Bible tells of wars and rumors of war:
The "News" is devastation on every side ...
War covers the globe ... some so near, others far,
The world is steeping in bloodshed, war's a raging tide;

His mind is wandering ... he sees loved ones back home,
Memories cluster and fuse in black bomb-filled air;
Familiar landmarks have disappeared and gone ...
Pain filled eyes ... except for rubble ... landscape bare.

A timed test! Must hurry ... for the clock ticks away,
As if awakening ... comes to himself with a start ...
He just must do better ... not let his mind stray;
Try as he will ... for this test he has no heart.

Peace and quiet seem worse than war, awaiting word;
Waiting and praying God someway will bring a halt,
And loved ones be safe at home where bombs are heard,
That God bring Judgment on those who are at fault.

War far or near ... faith assures our God does see,
God sent His Son to die ... His love was so strong:
    Christ came to die in our stead ... Salvation's free;
The Lord knows all those who do His children wrong.

The men who are in power will answer the more;
Choosing to the wage brutal war ... reckless of route ...
    Bring more heartache ... always isn't at the core
The disregard of life seems to ever mount.

While test answers get lost in war bomb debris,
Christ is the answer, in peace or war's waste:
    God forgives the sin of the repentant heart ...
In sorrow, come to the throne of God's Grace.

All-Time Favorites

Are You as Rich as I?
(A poem of the early 1950's)

A rich man while admiring his grand estate,
Was annoyed to see a beggar watching outside
   the gate.
He called to him to be on his way,
But, to his surprise, he made this reply,
Are you as rich as I?

You are rich in this world's goods,
You have your land, your mansion and money.
And I, though poor and shabbily dressed,
Will someday dwell in a mansion on high.
Are you as rich as I?

You worry and fret over problems of wealth,
   afraid of losing what you gained,
While I know my treasure is secure,
For in the skies, moth and rust doth not corrupt,
And thieves cannot enter in.
Are you as rich as I?

You are a nobleman of stately birth,
Of which titles and names are temporal.
By Spiritual Birth I am joint-heirs with Jesus
   Christ,
A child of the Heavenly King.
Are you as rich as I?

You, too, can be at peace with God,
And happy all the while,
If you'll accept the Christ who died,
And let Him within your heart abide.
You, too, can be as rich as I.

Sand and Pearls

Tribulation worketh patience ... Romans 5:3;
Patience, experience, and experience hope, a decree:
In Christ, hope maketh not ashamed, the love of God
Which is shed abroad, in hearts, by the Holy Ghost.

God's Spirit is given through Christ in Salvation;
For when we all were without strength, Christ died for us:
He shed His blood on Calvary for the ungodly ...
In love reaches to every one ... to you and me.

If when you pray, you sincerely ask for patience,
Don't be surprised ... if tribulation comes at once,
Trying of your faith, worketh patience: James 1:3;
In patience, perfect work, nothing wanting there'll be.

Because of irritation, the oyster makes a pearl;
A grain of sand, it works and around 'round to swirl;
Something of value made from irritating sand!
The oyster works within its bounds, with what's at hand.

Man born of woman ... few days and full of trouble;
Following God's plan, works won't be burned as stubble;
God's great Salvation's is a gift through Christ and it's free;
A life lived for Christ, like the pearl, beautiful can be.

Where are the Children?

Where are the children should be an o'erwhelming cry,
Many have gone in way of the dark day and blackest
    night;
Undisciplined, they wander where horrors creep and
    pounce,
In byways with gullies, muddy water, flooding waves,
Causing a struggle in hearts to tear and rend, while sight
    of despondency escapes;

While someone who understands and cares could ease the
    unease and fright,
By pointing the way, as to strangers, midst sand dunes
    wandering, seeking the right path.
Turning them on the right course, leading with wisdom,
    which comes from on high.
When that's seen pending, doing their best, to divert
    disaster.
By teaching children of Christ, therefore, a nobler way
    of life.

Where are the children, who in the future will lead?
Will there be any who for TRUTH unwaveringly stand,
As the strong oak, or will they be as reeds and shaken
    leaves ...
Who fall and wither from life's strenuous demands?
For children to be taught God's word, there's a need;

Learning of Christ, how He died on the cross, for man's
    sin;
God's Holy Spirit convicts the heart of man ...
The whole of the world's trouble, man needs understand,
In his refusing God's place of Salvation turning to
    his own creed;
Children learn what is a farce ... where Christ is truly
    exalted, they easily see.

A Mother's Legacy

(Lo, children are an heritage of the Lord,
and the fruit of the womb is His reward.) Psalms 127:3

Our children are on loan from God,
For their care, we'll answer to him;
"Old-fashioned" parents ... are not "mod!"
God's word teaches how to raise them.

In the nurture and admonition
Of the Lord ... to parents, a command;
A job considered menial to some;
Missing accolades so grand!

Listening for their cry, day and night;
Not nine to five, but, from sun to sun ...
Making light of what some call plight,
Still, making time to join their fun.

Always lodged in a true mother's heart,
Is teaching them what's good and right;
An obligation ... she feels her part ...
God's love, always, the depth and height.

The precepts, of the Lord when learned,
Will be recalled in later life ...
Whether in lowly circumstance
Or exalted ... with honor's rife.

Faith in Christ should be taught early;
It's never too soon to start ...
When understanding comes in time,
Love of Christ fills each tender heart.

When they are taught so soon from birth,
Teaching with words they understand,
That Jesus is the best of friends,
He died to save the souls of men.

As years pass, their faith will increase,
When taught, at first, what's important;
Faith won't always make troubles cease;
But, will give strength to make them stand.

Childhood lullabies sometimes sooth,
At times, so does rocking in a chair;
Security's in knowing Christ ...
And the Holy Spirit is near.

Man is few days ... full of troubles,
And they culminate with the years ...
Still, a life can be lived to the full;
With faith in God to calm life's fears.

A Mother's love will show in children,
By values she instills in them ...
Accepting Christ as their Saviour,
They'll spend eternity with Him.

Doing her best with what she has,
Providing for those in her care ...
Trusting in God to see them through;
Love goes where nothing else will dare.

Circumstances can't confine love;
Where there's faith, there is no limit.
Such love as this from above ...
And though a lifetime ... seems like minutes.

A soft silk dress or suit of fine serge,
Though nice, will soon be ragged and worn;
Where Scriptures will be in memory, verge ...
Guiding one who has been reborn.

When small, they learned John 3:16,
Saying it when they first could talk;
Was part of education deemed ...
Later to help life's maze to walk.

To protect them is love's design;
In Christ, they're covered by His blood;
All evil ... the devil's behind ...
But, his power checked by God above.

A Mother's legacy is what she's taught;
To her children ... her life does speak;
In good times or through hardships wrought,
Where with faith, it's God's will she seeks.

The Love of Money

(written Nov. 8, 1956)

The love of money is the root of all evil;
In God's word we are told.
For money, men lie, steal and kill,
What wouldn't man do for a dollar?

Pirates and robbers take that which is belonging to others,
Cause children to go hungry and cold.
This is a terrible crime we cry,
And should be punished for being so bold!

Alas! Stop! Think! Christian soul!
What values do you place on a dollar?
Does love of it come first in life?
And lack of it, cause torment and strife?

Do you neglect the word of God,
Do we lack missionaries to preach the word?
Does worldly gain come first with you,
Or to rescue some soul from satan?

Is the church-house run down?
Are the doors about to fall?
Are things left undone which should be done,
Because the offerings fall.

Is the preacher poorly paid?
Are the pews always empty?
For there's no time to worship God,
Another dollar is in the making!

Do you work six days a week, and overtime if needed,
Always there to punch the clock and never late at all,
But, on Sunday morning, always late IF you come at all.
It's queer that relaxation's needed on Sunday, worst of all.

When the collection plate is passed,
Do you really sacrifice?
Or does sacrifice mean to you,
Giving what is left after your spending is through!

Christ truly sacrificed His life for you,
Then will you use that term so loosely?
And describe the little you give,
We're still unprofitable servants, after we've done all that's
    our duty to do.

If you are stingy in your offerings to God,
And instead of the widow's mite,
You give what you might have left,
Then don't ask why, when, instead of blessings, God uses
His chastening rod!

Wake up! Dear Christian soul.
The love of money has taken its toll.
When we forget the house of God,
Then say, Oh, Lord I love thee so!

By withholding that which belongs to God,
You miss blessings which would be yours,
If you but place values where values belong!
And putting God first you can't go wrong!

For thirty pieces of silver, my Saviour was sold.
The love of money made Judas bold.
How Christ was betrayed is a story of old.

Christian soul, beware, lest your influence to
the devil is sold!

Mother

The word ... "Mother" ... seems so many
    different things.
Mother – to be mothers ... means much more
    than children and wedding rings;
Taking care – when children are babies is
    a responsibility filled with joy.
After a baby is born – it matters not
    whether it's a girl or boy.
As babies grow into toddlers ... everything
    they do is fun;
Although, as a mother you have no rest from
    the morn to setting sun.

Teaching children what's wrong and right –
    early on, should be done;
Parents' duty to see about ... mothers spend
    more time with little ones – no doubt.
The first few years of a child's life ...
    much is learned – not from sister or brother;
The values on which their life is based,
    comes from teachings of their mother.
Then, so many years of ... grade school, high school
    and college – even;
Many activities you participate in at school,
    fabric of your life weaving.

So ... a "Mother" is a " Mother," no matter her
    age – or your age either!
She doesn't always look at you ... and judge
    as others gauge
Remember, it take much more than having a
    baby, to be a mother!
If she takes her job seriously, as God –

expects ... much easier to be someone – other!
She needs to love, always ...supportive and
     encourage –;
A true mother's love – will never desire,
     to disparage.

No matter diversity of position, others may
     hold;
A mother's job is paramount, with duties
     manifold;
To love and scold, to encourage good morals
     and ideals ... lofty,
Be strong in the Lord ... life's full of hard
     knocks – no room for a softie!
At times, not understanding ... only human –
     allowing for mistakes;
One thing you can know ... true "Mother"
     love can never be fake!

Love Hides

The Bible tells us ... love hides a multitude of
    sins ...;
Overlooking what's considered another's fault
    speaks well of you;
We're not to compromise the truths ... but, stand
    for right, in our compassion –;
While with wisdom and understanding, we grant
    all the dignity that's due.

Love never vaunts itself ... or behaves itself
    unseemly ... at another's expense;
To validate how intelligent one may be...
    mattering not – no wisdom is spent;
Love never casts down with nothing constructive
    for action ... hence ...;
Love doesn't resent another's accomplishment ...
    perhaps, to you, not lent.

Hiding a multitude of sins ... means overlooking ...
    not stirring up strife –;
To love ... is to always have the benefit of the
    other in mind ...;
Criticism that isn't constructive ... everywhere
    is rife;
Yet, hearts that love and care ... crosses of
    another will bear – for love does bind.

Life
(An Early Poem)

Life without the Lord is empty,
Dreary, futile, 'tis an empty shell.
And full of heartache, pain and sorrow,
For the wayward soul, on his road to hell.

Life with Christ is full and fruitful,
If we but follow His Holy Word,
We have peace, contentment, pleasures,
As we strive to serve our Lord.

May we who know the Saviour's Love,
Not hinder those who would seek His face above,
But, let our lives so consecrated be,
That a poor lost sinner in a darkened world, a ray of light
    may see.

Believe the Lord – (written Dec. 4, 1960)

Believe the Lord in all His promises.
His word is true; He'll see you through
    every trial and misfortune.
Never falter in the way, where the Lord is leading.
Though rough the road with many thorns
    to pierce you.

Christ, our Lord, is the companion who
    stays close to your side to protect,
        lest the thorns prick too deeply.
Troubles only draw us nearer His side,
    so He can comfort, and we'll desire
        in His Will to abide.
His love is shown in many ways
    if we only take time to meditate upon
The blessings He gives every day.

We don't deserve His matchless love,
Only God's grace sent Christ from
    above to die the terrible death He died.
To save my soul, He was crucified.
All He asks is that I believe for Salvation,
    that will last for eternity.

I believe my Lord on high; give me
    grace to live for Thee while here on
        earth, and may, if needed, die for Thee
In love, as Thou didst die for me.
Let my life mean no more to me
    than Thine to Thee, when you gave it on
Calvary, to save my soul and set me free.

I believe.

Looking Back

Happy Anniversary
(Cinquain)

I loved
You from the start ...
Life's mountains and valleys,
Bringing joy and hurt, have not changed ...
My heart!

Looking Forward

Forever
(Cinquain)

I love
You ... I do! The
Years are more than three score;
Only Heaven will let me love ...
You more.

Anniversary Poem
For: Carl

And here is Ho-Bo, our little dog, the poem "Unconditional Love" is dedicated to ... sitting in the midst of all Mother's books he so faithfully helped with — proudly "surveying his kingdom." On February 1st, 2021 our dear little friend, Ho-Bo, passed through the "doggie gates" of Heaven. He is missed.